The Secrets of the
Dolls' House
Makers

The Secrets of the
Dolls' House
Makers

Jean Nisbett

GUILD OF MASTER CRAFTSMAN PUBLICATIONS LTD

First published 1994 by
Guild of Master Craftsman Publications Ltd,
166 High Street, Lewes,
East Sussex BN7 1XU

© Jean Nisbett 1994

ISBN 0 946819 54 8

Designed by Teresa Dearlove

Printed in Hong Kong by H. Y. Printing Co.

Photo Acknowledgements
Jean Nisbett and the Guild of Master Craftsman Publications gratefully acknowledge the following people and
agencies for granting us permission to reproduce their photographs in *The Secrets of the Dolls' House Makers*.
The photographs on the following pages were supplied courtesy of:
Gordon Blacklock pp 126–29; David Booth pp 68–71; Jeremy Collins p 98 (top right, bottom);
Michael Crockett pp 88, 93; John Davenport pp 1, 72–75, 77; Ann Davey p 3 (bottom); Beatrice Dopita pp 149–153;
Judith Dunger p 2; EMF Publishing (Dolls House & Miniature Scene) p 36; Richard Goddard pp 154–59;
Guild of Master Craftsman pp 18 (bottom), 19, 35, 96, 97, 98 (top left); Hever Castle Ltd pp 172–79;
Edward Hill pp 130–35; Michelle Hipkins pp 136–141; Barry Hipwell pp 84–87; Bob Hopwood pp 142, 143, 145, 147;
Charlotte Hunt pp 89–92; Carol Lodder p 148; Peter Mattinson pp 6–11; Reg Miller pp 12–17;
John & Jean Morgan pp 94, 95; Kevin Mulvany pp 20–23; Steve Orino p 18 (top); Ken Palmer pp 144, 160–63;
Michael and Edwards Partners p 3 (top and middle); Patrick Puttock pp 100–05;
Colin & Yvonne Roberson p 111; Gordon & Joyce Rossiter pp 24–29; Brian & Eileen Rumble pp 30–34;
Terence Stringer pp 168, 171 (bottom); Robert Stubbs pp 37–41; Titchfield Studios Ltd p 76;
Bernardo Traettino pp 43–46, 47 (top); Ivan Turner pp 113–117; John Watkins pp 61, 62, 64 (top);
Trevor Webster pp 48–53; David Whitehead pp 78–83; Martin Williams p 112;
Geoffrey Wonnacott pp 118–123; Ellie Yannas pp 54–59

Front cover photograph © Andrew Kolesnikow.
The photograph is of the Diana Gallery, from the Palace of Fontainebleau. The miniature palace, by
Mulvany & Rogers, is on permanent exhibition at Carol and Barry Kaye's Museum of Miniature Art in Los Angeles.

Acknowledgements

would like to thank the craftspeople who have given their time to talk to me and supplied photographs of their work, and to Hever Castle Ltd for allowing me to reproduce the photographs of John Hodgson's Georgian house from the Guthrie Miniature Model House Collection.

I am also grateful to my husband, whose scientific background enabled him to make clear to me some of the technical processes described, and also for his additional photography.

Thanks are also due to my editor, Elizabeth Inman, for her efficiency and enthusiasm, which have allowed the book to be produced in a remarkably short space of time, and to Teresa Dearlove, the book's designer, for the attractive format.

Contents

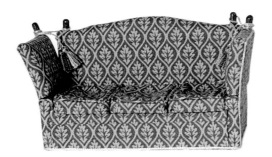

Part Three
Decorative
Objects

Introduction

The dolls' house hobby is a twentieth-century phenomenon which has grown rapidly over the past decade to become a major leisure pursuit. Interest first spread from the United States to Britain at a time when most people still thought of dolls' houses purely as children's toys. The increasing demand for hand-crafted dolls' houses, furniture and accessories in the recognized international collector's scale of 1/12 has persuaded many craftspeople to try using their skills to satisfy this new market.

Elaborate period-style dolls' houses attract widespread interest. Photographs of outstanding, individually commissioned dolls' houses appear in national newspapers and magazines, with details about their makers, the number of hours work which went into the creation of these masterpieces, and sometimes the staggering amount reached at auction in aid of charity. The hobby has spread to the Continent, where, as in Britain and the United States, dolls' house fairs, exhibitions and specialist shops continue to increase in number.

Dolls' houses are only part of this creative industry, which includes furniture of many periods, textiles, glass, porcelain, pottery and

One of England's finest miniaturists, Denis Hillman has made a speciality of French furniture. This Louis XVI cupboard commode, known as a dauphin cabinet, is a copy of one commissioned for the dauphin and bears the royal cypher. The miniature has a working lock and marble top. Denis was one of the first people to begin making fine replicas in 1/12 scale and has been an inspiration to other miniaturists.

many small accessories to complete the perfect miniature interior. Specialist craftspeople make everything from a silver-topped cane to an Art Deco vase. The range and quality of today's miniature work is astonishing and guarantees appeal to a wide public.

This book celebrates the work of some of the foremost craftspeople working in the miniature scale today. To anyone who has not yet entered this small world, the pictures of these dolls' houses and miniatures will be a revelation. We can only marvel at the skills of the makers of these architecturally accurate dolls' houses, and the exquisite detail of the furniture and accessories.

These makers came to their specialist work by diverse routes. A few began immediately after training in art or architecture, sidetracked from their full-size ambitions. Some were made redundant from their previous job, decided to use skills in a new way, and have made a success of it. Others retired and wanted to tackle something different which they had always intended to do when they had the time. All have something in common: a passionate interest in their work and the willingness to experiment until working in 1/12 scale became as natural as regular size. In

1

original, in your own distinctive style. There is always room for a new maker of versatility and real talent – but it may also help to be in the right place at the right time. At a dolls' house fair I once overheard someone ask, 'Where can I find an Art Nouveau dolls' house? It's a period which fascinates me.' Exhibiting for the first time at that fair was a young partnership from Cumbria, showing an elegant Art Nouveau-style house. They took their first order and the next few months' work was assured.

If you want to make dolls' houses or miniatures purely for pleasure, perhaps for your own family or friends, you can work at your own pace and avoid the pressures of a competitive market. But watch out – if you learn

Left This longcase clock by Judith Dunger is copied from one *circa* 1720 and has a working movement and pendulum.
  Judith 'japans', her furniture in the same way as the eighteenth-century English craftsmen, using goldleaf and raised gesso work to imitate oriental lacquer. The style of decoration was known as chinoiserie and became immensely popular. Judith's furniture is made for her by her father, Bernard Burton, an antiques restorer.

Below The Chinese Chippendale- style chair is 3¼in high; the pole screen on a tripod stand is adjustable in height to shield the sitter from the heat of the fire.

a size where 1in is equivalent to 1ft (i.e. 1cm represents 12cm), an error of ¹⁄₃₂in (.08mm) is a mistake of gross proportions. One moment's lapse in concentration at any stage can mean starting all over again. Craftspeople working in such a small size need to be both practical and innovative; it may, for example, be necessary to adapt and sometimes invent tools and reinvent working methods. Artistic imagination and craft skill of a high order are both essential.The helpful information and advice they give will inspire both the amateur and anyone aiming for a professional career in miniatures.

If you want to sell, you will need to find a gap in the market, to make something

2

Right **The Round House**, in Art Nouveau style, by Michael & Edwards Partners, opens in two halves, allowing each internal floor to rotate about the central spiral staircase. Interior glass partitions and decorative window panels create a light, open display for miniature furniture, and the Art Nouveau style is reinforced by delicate brass etching.

Bottom right Ann Davey uses the Tudor rose and the strawberry in this quilt. Both were incorporated into the embroideries of the time wherever possible. Both the coverlet and the stitches are in pure silk.

how to make something unique which the miniature world is crying out for, you may find that you have another career open to you whether you intended it or not. Some of the makers featured in this book began in this way.

Dolls' houses can change your life. Recently an elderly visitor, in her eighties, came to see my dolls' house collection. At first she was surprised that none of them were antique, and looked slightly doubtful. I opened a house and offered her a seat in front of it. She sat for a long time without saying a word. Eventually she turned and said, 'There's a whole world here which I

never knew existed. I have found a new interest.'

I hope that others will be as intrigued as she was by the work of the miniature makers, and that those with the capacity to develop special skills will be encouraged to try working in the small scale. You never know what you can do until you try.

3

Part One

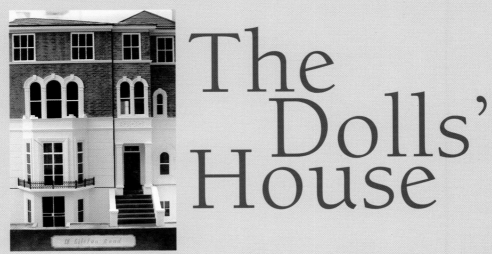

The Dolls' House

Peter Mattinson
The Architectural Approach

Peter Mattinson's speciality is to reproduce period architecture in dolls' houses with the patina of age and the atmosphere of a building which is steeped in history. If he makes a dolls' house based on a still-existing sixteenth-century building, then the dolls' house, too, will look as if it had been made in the sixteenth century, with all the evidence of worn carving, gently undulating roof, slightly leaning walls, and paved floors which have been eroded by the footsteps of many generations.

In York, where he lives, there is plenty to inspire him, as he has a special affinity with Tudor and Jacobean houses, although he also makes houses which reproduce those of many periods, from Tudor to Victorian. He enjoys getting to work on period detail, whether it is the mellowed brick and weathered beams of a country manor, or the marble stairs, decorative plasterwork and Corinthian pillars in a Georgian town house. He prefers to work on a building with plenty of depth to its surface, not just a plain, flat facade.

His original intention was to be a photographer, but when he realized the difficulties of earning a living in his early days as a freelance, he decided to learn a practical trade first, and took a job as a trainee carpenter and joiner. Not only did he become a first-rate craftsman, but he also had the opportunity to work on period properties, which sparked off his initial interest in old buildings.

While doing renovation work he made a point of finding out exactly how each house had been constructed, and how successive owners had altered the building from the original plan. He found it instructive, too, to be able to study the way in which wear and tear over the years had affected the various building materials.

After this spell as a carpenter and joiner, Peter began work with a firm of quantity

Left **Work in progress on the front of the Goodramgate house, before the addition of the ancient-looking carved porch.**

Right **The interior of the Goodramgate house complete with medieval wall paintings.**

surveyors. This was good training in method. He always records the techniques that he has used on each dolls' house, and the list of processes he has gone through to produce the final effect, as well as the costings for the materials used. He likes to build a dolls' house, wherever possible, in the same way as the full-size house, using the correct sequence of construction and methods of jointing, and then work backwards, undoing the pristine finish of his newly completed, architecturally accurate model. He takes photographs of the houses he makes at each stage in their construction, and keeps a record of each specially mixed paint shade and the colours that he uses on each house. This means that he can reproduce exactly the same shades if a customer wants an addition to a previous commission.

Peter became involved with dolls' houses when he was shown one made by a friend, and thought that he might enjoy making one himself. By chance, he then saw a dolls' house maker through a workshop window, and went in to ask for some advice on what

he thought of as just a new hobby at that time, to add to photography and painting.

Once he had found out the correct scale to use, discovered how many people were involved with the dolls' house hobby, and tried out some of his initial ideas, he then went to some dolls' house and miniatures fairs and discussed these ideas with miniaturists he met there. Everyone was generous with help and information, he recalls, and he was encouraged by useful advice from Caroline Hamilton, the organizer

of the London Dollshouse Festival. Peter worked hard at perfecting his techniques in miniature work and was invited to show in London.

His innovative style attracted a great deal of attention, and commissions followed. Even so, he cautiously kept on his regular job; giving up steady employment to rely on the vagaries of freelance work would have been a big step. But after making dolls' houses for several years on a part-time basis, Peter realized that he really did have a product that people wanted. In contrast, the work for his firm of surveyors was dwindling as recession began to bite, and he decided eventually to turn to full-time dolls' house making. One advantage of working in miniature scale, he says, is that you don't need a large workshop and can work from home, saving overheads.

Research and planning are essential: he begins by taking a series of photographs, and then likes to check out unusual period features in detail through books, visits to

museums, and sometimes through local history records about the original house. Most old houses have been altered at some stage, some many times, and very few are as they were when built. If a later addition is an anachronism or does not complement the

In general, he doesn't use tools specifically designed for miniature work, but prefers to work with his regular tools. 'After all,' he says, 'it is a full-size hand that is holding the tool and doing the work.' Despite the apparent complexity of his

A carved oak chair and chest for one of Peter's Tudor interiors.

earlier period, Peter will revert to the original plan, especially with the interior layout. However, if the extensions and alterations are in keeping and add to the character of the house, these will be included in the model. For example, an early house may have had a large chimneystack built on, and such a feature can be attractive.

Peter stresses that the key to success as a dolls' house maker is to think things through carefully at the start. Ten hours spent at the planning stage, making scale drawings of every detail and working out things like floor levels and access to rooms, can save 50 hours' work at a later stage, and means that you can be sure of achieving what you intend.

finished work, he prefers to keep his methods and techniques as simple as possible. He will use standard machinery in an unorthodox way, rather than fill up his workshop with too much machinery which can only be used for occasional, specialized jobs.

He does, however, make quite a few of his own handtools, particularly for carving. Astonishingly, his favourite tool is a small, old plastic screwdriver which came from a Christmas cracker. He sharpened it up and finds it perfect for achieving carved detail. 'Once you have found a technique which really works for you,' he says, 'stay with it.'

Carving is one of Peter's great pleasures. He will spend days carving a jetty, and then a few more hours knocking it about – but with great care and skill – to make it look worn and battered in precisely the way the original might have weathered.

He uses both plywood and medium density fibreboard (MDF) in his models, the choice depending on how the material is to be incorporated into a structure. One disadvantage of MDF for structural purposes is that it tends to crack when you screw into it, whereas plywood, with its layered cross-grain, holds together better. With a timber-framed house he builds in the traditional way, the framing constructed first and then infilled.

He uses professional artists' paints for any special effects, because the pigments are well dispersed and will hold the true colour without variation once a shade has been mixed. For larger areas of paint he always uses trade-quality house paints, as they are generally superior to those available to the amateur.

Peter buys in very little in the way of ready made mouldings, preferring to create his own. For example, he will carve a length of egg-and-dart cornice individually, in precise facsimile of the original, then using this as a master, will make a mould and cast enough to complete a room. If an original feature was made in wood, not plaster, he feels strongly that it should be reproduced only in wood, which has a completely different feeling from plasterwork. He may not use the same type of wood as in, for example, full-size panelling, but chooses one which will give the exact effect of the scaled-down grain of the original.

He makes such things in metal as hinges, unusual door furniture and light fittings. 'My

A marble and gilt side table of a type very popular around 1740. Henry Flitcroft, William Kent , Matthias Lock and Nicholas Pineau – on whose design this table is based – all produced similar elaborate and impressive tables.

metalwork classes at school really came in useful,' he says. But he will buy in a well-made 1/12 scale Victorian doorknocker or bell push if he knows that he really does require a standard fitting. Lighting is something that he has found to be straightforward, provided it is planned carefully, and he likes to design and make his own individual light fittings if they are needed.

To complete some of his interiors, he has made miniature versions of some impressive eighteenth-century decorative furniture. His side table with marble top and gilded, elaborately carved apron and legs, is a splendid example of an ornate rococo style. This lingered on into the late eighteenth century in furniture mainly designed by architects when a room was conceived as a whole.

The gilded metal base for the table is cast for him from his own handcarved master. But he doesn't leave it just gilded – he carefully whites down the gilding to suggest the effect of the gessowork of the original table. He also uses a mould to cast the table tops in black-coloured resin, which is then marbled with green veining.

In a natural progression from making dolls' houses, Peter is often asked to provide some of the furniture – if only because no one else would 'age' a piece as he does, an effect which is essential if the whole house and contents are to be consistent in style. This is particularly evident in his Tudor and Jacobean furniture, which is lovingly carved and, of course, incorporates the effect of wear and tear which he feels has become his trademark.

Reg Miller
The Traditionalist

Reg Miller's dolls' houses are an artist's impression of period, but created three-dimensionally in wood rather than painted on canvas. He has a variety of magnificent 1/12 scale houses to his credit, and they are solid enough for play. He *wants* them to be used and handled, so that the owner can actively share his pleasure in creating a complete evocation of a whole period.

Reg's interest in the miniature scale began during a holiday when he saw 'cabinet', or 'baby' houses in German and Dutch museums. His first cabinet house, Stuart Lodge, has a polished wooden exterior. The facade is complete with all the correct architectural detail for the period 1600–1650, but from the outside it really looks more like a piece of furniture than a dolls' house. When opened up, however, it displays coffered ceilings, panelled walls and doors, elaborate cornices and a magnificent staircase, all incredibly detailed.

Reg also likes to introduce an element of mystery into his houses, and the Jacobean period is rich with opportunities for this. Behind the panelling in Stuart Lodge is a secret staircase, which can be glimpsed when a concealed door is opened at the side of a fireplace. Although it can never be seen in its entirety, Reg has the satisfaction of knowing that every detail of that hidden stairway is as perfect as the rooms in full view in front of it. He found that for a spare-time activity his painstaking construction of this Jacobean-style cabinet house was both absorbing and rewarding, so when he took early retirement in 1980, he decided to combine his love of architecture, painting and history with his practical skills as a woodworker, and make dolls' houses full time for adults.

Although he never intended to become a full-time lecturer, Reg spent 25 years teaching art and history of art. After gaining a degree in fine art, his work was considered so outstanding that he went on to the Royal College of Art, but in the the post-war period it was difficult to become recognized, and many aspiring young artists took on a certain amount of teaching work to help pay their way. He also dabbled in the theatre for a while, working as a freelance designer, and continued to paint as well. When he married, he accepted the stability of a permanent job as a lecturer and, later, with a family to look after, he decided to stay in the academic world when an even better-paid post was offered.

Reg's woodworking skills were honed as a result of his progress up the career ladder. With each successive appointment, the Miller family moved to a different part of the country. The need to learn woodworking in order to improve the different period houses they lived in gave Reg useful experience for his later occupation. Tackling a variety of tasks allowed him to exercise both technique and manual skills. He discovered that work which at first seemed difficult was really quite straightforward if each task was approached methodically, even if it meant

taking something to pieces to see how it had been put together originally.

After retirement, Reg and his wife moved to Yorkshire, to an Edwardian house on the edge of the moors. This one was spacious enough to allow him to do more practical work, and to introduce some changes of his own – he converted two rooms into one to form a 30ft workshop. Reg loves working in wood, and he uses a lot of it. He cut up 1½cwt (78kg) of pine to make Stuart Lodge, which is 4ft 6in (1.38m) high, and weighs ¾cwt (38kg). He likes to use unstained pine which, when polished, will gradually deepen to a warm honey colour.

His houses are all based to some extent

on a real building, and his first step is always to take dozens of photographs before drawing the floor plan for his model. He works out the height of each room, and then calculates the sizes of architraves, doors, fireplaces, windows and archways, exactly to scale. He makes wooden templates for all these basic mouldings, and when the house is finished all the templates are kept in his workshop, strung together, as a record of each individual part he made for the house.

His attention to detail is total. His casement and sash windows all work. Floors are given a final sanding with the edge of a piece of glass for extra smoothness. The wood grain for each panel or floorboard is selected with great care so that each section matches the next well, and there are no out-of-scale knots. He uses a Stanley knife for scratch mouldings and a scalpel for carving architraves. But it is perhaps his staircases which are most impressive. The balusters are all individually turned – yet a large staircase may have 150 balusters and they must all match precisely, as the slightest difference will show up badly. He may need to make 200 to achieve 150 which meet his high standards. That kind of challenge might be exasperating, but when the staircase is successfully completed, he feels that it really is an achievement he can be proud of.

One of his worst moments came when making such a staircase. It was all finished and he was fitting on the handrail when he realized it was slightly skewed. As he made his final adjustment he managed to snap off the beautifully shaped curve at the bottom, which had taken him so much time and trouble to make, and the handrail had to be remade.

Reg's original training as an artist means that his houses are not left entirely in unadorned polished wood. He emphasizes particular elements in order to create arresting features which will contrast with the

Left **The main staircase of the Northumberland hall house.**

Below **The interior of Argyll House,** *circa* **1720, with the delightful Chinese bedroom.**

Bottom **A more detailed view of the Chinese bedroom in Argyll House.**

finely carved wooden interiors. The 'marble' floors and fireplace surrounds are not always what they seem, for, as in earlier ages, the effect of marble is often simulated in paint on wood.

Argyll House is a good example of an eighteenth-century house with a papered room to reflect the vogue at that time for chinoiserie. Although an appropriate wrapping paper can represent a scaled-down version of a Chinese wallpaper, Reg does not put it on as it is. He cuts and reassembles parts of the design to make a balanced picture which exactly suits the size and shape of the space to be filled. He rubs away at the back of the pieces to be applied until

the paper is so thin that when glued into place the join is invisible. The striking Chinese bedroom in Argyll House is papered in this manner. Reg considered handpainting a wallpaper design, but felt that this method reproduced the texture of a miniaturized Chinese wallpaper more exactly in the small scale.

Not all his houses are cabinet houses. His most extensive has taken years to build, in 11 separate sections. It is based on a hall house in the Northumberland vernacular

style, dating from around 1700 but extended by each succeeding generation. In the Victorian and Edwardian periods the addition of wings for the ever-increasing number of servants meant that the later additions almost surrounded the original building. When his customer first enquired if he would like to copy a real building, Reg was told it was 'an extended Northumberland cottage', which indeed it was – but when he arrived to photograph it, he wondered whether he had brought enough rolls of film. He had not been told that the south and east wings had each been extended to over 100ft (30m), in addition to the central block.

But whatever commission he is offered, Reg seems eventually to return to his first love, the cabinet house. One of his favourites is his Highgrove 'baby' house, based on Prince Charles' Gloucestershire home as it had been long before Prince Charles took up

residence. Reg had seen a photograph of the house in *Country Life* magazine, as it was when occupied by Maurice Macmillan, and was attracted to the fairly plain but beautifully proportioned exterior. He has never seen inside, but took as his starting point the typical layout of an English eighteenth-century 'baby' house.

Reg likes nothing better than being asked to provide the furniture for a house, too, as this will complete his 'vision' of the period.

Far left **The south elevation of the Northumberland hall house,** *circa* **1720.**

Left **The impressive entrance hall of the Highgrove 'baby' house, with marble floor and pillars, simulated in paint.**

Below left **Highgrove 'baby' house,** *circa* **1797. The house opens in three sections and contains a secret staircase.**

Below **Part of a set of finely carved William and Mary chairs.**

Right **Hooper's saddler's shop,** *circa* **1790. The wrought iron balconies and pavement grilles which can be lifted out were made by John Watkins (see page 60).**

Sets of chairs are a particular delight, where he again relishes the difficulties involved in making identical carvings. The more complicated, the better, he says – it is a mixture of frustration and pleasure.

Although the original craftsmen also had to make near-identical sets of carvings by hand, they had an advantage over Reg: in full size you cannot look at the detail on six chairs all at once, whereas in 1/12 scale as little as 1/64in (less than half a millimetre) discrepancy will be glaringly obvious. This smallness makes Reg's task 12 times harder.

My own favourite amongst Reg's houses is a shop with living accommodation above, a replica of a late-eighteenth-century saddler's shop, commissioned by its present owner. The original shop was built in red brick, but at the customer's request the copy is reproduced in the attractive pale yellow of London stock brick when new. The miniature brickwork is scored into the solid pine, and then painted. Inside, Reg really enjoyed creating an interior as it might have been around 1890. It was to be designed to suit an imaginary retired army officer who had taken to shopkeeping in that period, and the difference of 100 years between the building and its later use makes an interesting contrast.

The shop is furnished with mahogany, glass-fronted cupboards, and a mahogany counter with glass shelves and top. Reg used his own handmade frosted glass for the cupboard front. He has found that the best way to make frosted glass to suit 1/12 scale is to rub 1/12in (2mm) thick glass with wet-and-dry abrasive papers until it creates a frosting of the desired texture.

The seventeenth and eighteenth centuries are Reg's favourite periods for furniture, but he has also built houses from much earlier times. One of these is adapted from the house immortalized by Beatrix Potter in *The Tailor of Gloucester*.

This enchanting little house (now a shop), in a tiny street near Gloucester Cathedral, makes the ideal miniature building. Instead of the black-and-white timber-framed exterior which exists today, Reg has used beech for the wooden framing, contrasting with the lighter colour of the pine which represents plaster infilling. The interior has oak beams and oak floors, and the latches on the doors are made of oxidized silver. In the tradition of the cabinet house, every detail is exquisitely finished.

To Reg, time seems unimportant. He never considers how long something is going to take, but does everything as well as he can without counting the hours. He no longer has to cope with the pressures of earning enough to support a growing family, and most of his reward lies in creating a masterpiece which he knows will last for generations.

17

Mulvany & Rogers
Miniature Splendour

Kevin Mulvany and Susan Rogers are the best-known dolls' house building partnership in Britain. When they take on a commission, they aim to make an architecturally correct model with all the appropriate period detail, but without slavishly copying the exact layout. They use their combined creative talents to design miniature masterpieces that also work as dolls' houses in which the rooms are almost all open to view at one time. This may mean leaving out some of the minor rooms and concentrating on the most important. However, their rearrangement to suit the dolls' house plan is always worked out on the same basis as the original. They want to recreate the feeling of a home for people to live in, however grand the decorations.

In 1992 their representation in 1/12 scale of the Palace of Versailles, commissioned by the Angels Attic Museum, in California, achieved national news coverage on television and was featured in newspapers and interior decorating magazines. The Palace as it exists today has been extended to contain approaching a thousand rooms – even the most elaborate replica could only include a small selection. Kevin and Susan decided that their miniature version would feature nine main rooms and several anterooms, reproducing the most

spectacular features of the original: the imposing entrance hall with its grand double staircase, the Hall of Mirrors, and the extravagantly decorated bedrooms for the king and queen. The magnificence of the dolls' house Versailles is awe-inspiring, and awe is exactly the feeling that Louis XIV, the Sun King, wanted to inspire in his courtiers.

Their version of Versailles took 11 months to make. It measures 82in wide,

decorative detail includes *trompe l'oeil* marble columns and gilded mouldings. The exterior has lead-covered dormers made in lead foil and cast replicas of stone-carved details.

Mulvany & Rogers aim for excellence in every detail, and they prefer to commission lighting, wrought ironwork and furniture from specialist makers, while they concentrate on making the house and producing the exquisite paint effects which make their houses unique.

Kevin and Susan met while studying for degrees in history of art and architecture, and married shortly afterwards, although Susan retains her original surname for professional purposes. They enjoyed making models, and after restoring a battered 1930s-style, 1/16 scale, commercially made children's dolls' house, they went on to make a simple Georgian-style dolls' house in 1/12 scale. That first house sold for £90 at a local craft fair, which at the time seemed a good return for their efforts. They then made another house in that style which they exhibited at a dolls' house and miniatures fair. This led to orders from several dolls' house shops, and also to their first commission direct from a collector, which provided just the opportunity they needed to miniaturize more elaborate architectural detail and period decorations. At this point, they realized that they could combine their

42in deep and 59in high (2.1m x 1.1m x 1.5m). There are 574 feet (175m) of ¼in (6mm) wide lime wood in the flooring – the parquet flooring in one room alone contains 3,500 individually cut pieces of wood, assembled in an intricate design. The

individual skills in a career partnership, with Kevin as architect and house builder, while Susan concentrated on the painting.

To help make ends meet when they were just beginning, Kevin took a three-month job at Shepperton Film Studios, making models for film sets. There, he learned that in film studios you have to work quickly, to a deadline, and not put time, effort and money into what nobody sees. He learned how to make up carcases of basic materials, to assemble them with strong, slot-in joints, and put a veneer of detail on top. He also discovered how to make moulds to reproduce handcarved architectural features in plaster or resin; this technique was to prove invaluable.

Since 1987 Kevin and Susan have never looked back. When they receive a commission they begin by visiting the house they are going to miniaturize and, after obtaining permission, they photograph the rooms from all angles and sketch every detail that they will need to reproduce. In addition, Susan paints colour samples for later reference.

Kevin then draws out very detailed plans for the model and only when they have agreed together on the precise layout does he start on the woodwork. He uses medium density fibreboard (MDF), because it does not distort and is suitable for the slot-in groove construction he uses. The smooth surface is also ideal for painted decoration.

A dolls' house in its simplest form begins as a box. Basically, Kevin makes a series of box sections to be jointed together and then they both set to work to cover everything up with paint and architectural additions. But there are simple boxes and

complicated ones; one of their houses may contain 40 rooms and have 20 internal doors. The miniature Versailles has 30 windows, of which seven are 'blind'. (A blind window is often as necessary in a dolls' house, as it was in many houses built in the eighteenth century, for perfect exterior symmetry.)

Kevin uses standard power tools to construct the carcase of a house: a hand-held jigsaw and a belt sander (both from a DIY store, but of the best quality available), a Minicraft model-making drill with attachments for carving and grinding, and a Black and Decker Workmate. His favourite tool is a Stanley knife and he also uses a variety of files and clamps, screwdrivers (which he sometimes sharpens to use as carving tools), and a razor saw and small mitre block.

He may spend days carving a particularly intricate length of cornice as a one-off special feature, and finds ramin the best wood to work on for this purpose. Repetitive mouldings for both exterior and interior, such as pillars and corbels, are all cast from master originals which Kevin hand-carves in

Opposite **A chandelier made for the Palace of Versailles by Donald and Robert Ward.**

Below **Work in progress on Het Loo, a William and Mary Dutch palace.**

plastic wood or car-body filler (useful because it has no grain and does not split). He makes a reusable rubber mould so that he can produce a set of identical mouldings in styrene, which takes a paint finish well.

Both Kevin and Susan take a share in the painting, although Susan is the specialist in *trompe l'oeil* (the art of painting views and objects to make them appear three-dimensional). The interior of a Mulvany & Rogers' house is always breathtaking. Gilded detail needs to have a raised effect, as it is copied from plasterwork, and Susan painstakingly and very gradually builds up the surface of her design, using tweezers to add minute dots of Milliput modelling compound and adding to the effect with wood glue (PVA) dripped on to make a series of tiny layers. She spends hours carving

minute detail with her favourite tool, a scalpel, which she deliberately blunts. The trouble with using a sharp scalpel, she says, is that the cutting edge wears very quickly on this type of work, and as you change from a blunt one to a new blade it is easy to make a mistake.

As many as five washes or glazes of watered-down acrylic paints can be used to achieve the exact finish needed – the Hall of Mirrors in Versailles needed seven to get it just right. Susan uses artists' gilding varnish, never gold paint, which would look over-bright. Nor does she ever use expensive paint brushes, as with this type of work they wear out so quickly. Instead, she prefers to work with cheap synthetic ones which she will throw away as soon as they show the slightest sign of wear.

Left Susan's *trompe l'oeil* decoration of the staircase landing in Malmaison features clouds in a blue sky, a very popular effect in eighteenth-century interiors. An example of curtains simulated in paint is also seen here.

Above right The exterior of Malmaison with its elaborate entrance canopy.

Below right Neoclassical painted decoration in the Parrot Room from Sturehof, Sweden. This room was made for Charlotte Hunt (*see* page 88), who added painted panels which include the parrot which gives the room its name.

Kevin and Susan want to achieve the feeling of the mature, original building, not a newly decorated version. Both agree that in 1/12 scale, you have to lose just a little of the sharpness of the original to make the decorations realistic; realism in miniature needs a gentler effect, a slightly softer finish.

Many decorative effects, such as marble floors and pillars, are painted, as might be expected. More surprisingly, Susan often simulates curtains in paint. Draping material always causes problems in this scale, as it never lies quite flat enough – or drapes in the same way – as in full size. Woodblock floors are another special feature. Kevin uses lime to reproduce an oak parquet floor, and stains it in imitation of oak, as lime has a very fine grain, which in 1/12 scale gives a better simulation of the appearance of oak. Mahogany can be used in full-size flooring because the grain of the wood is not so obvious.

Kevin and Susan have also miniaturized Malmaison, the private palace which Napoleon shared with Josephine and gave to her on their divorce. The replica is only one-room deep and the collector who had commissioned it had asked that it should include a double-height room. When they visited the real Malmaison, which is now a museum, Kevin and Susan found that the ceilings were of no more than average height throughout, so they adapted their design to incorporate the taller Salon of the Four Seasons from the Hotel de Beauharnais in Paris. This building, like Malmaison, was designed by Charles Percier and Pierre Fontaine, so the change seemed permissible artistic licence. Kevin used the original architectural drawings by Percier and Fontaine to copy in wood the intricate design of the wood-and-metal entrance canopy which is such a spectacular feature of the otherwise plain exterior of the palace.

Every house they make is based on a real building, but sometimes, as with Malmaison, they will add especially interesting

architectural features taken from another house of the same period at the request of the customer. Both agree that their favourite period is broadly defined as anything from 1600 to 1800, although they will tackle something outside this if it is a real challenge.

They say they cannot envisage reproducing a modern house because, for them, it just would not have enough texture and surface interest, and in any case an exact replica with crisp, modern detailing might appear like an architect's model. They like to work on something which inspires their feeling for period and historical accuracy.

Gordon & Joyce Rossiter

The Builders

 hen Gordon Rossiter first started making miniature houses, he already had all the basic skills at his fingertips. He had spent 27 years running his own building firm in Dorchester, constructing full-scale houses using tried and tested methods, and employing workmen with an ingrained understanding and appreciation of traditional skills. Seeing modern, time-saving methods filtering into the building trade, Gordon began to feel that soon all houses would be built in prefabricated sections unloaded from the back of a lorry, with no need for the skills of his plumbers, joiners and carvers. An idea formed at the back of his mind that he would like to build a model of a traditional Dorset house, as a permanent record of traditional building methods.

After settling on early retirement, Gordon

planned to start work on the model house, but first he and his wife Joyce decided it was time for a sabbatical. After an extended holiday in France, they took another trip, this time to Cumbria and Yorkshire, and it was while exploring the Yorkshire Dales that they visited a dolls' house and miniatures fair – and discovered 1/12 scale. The realization that so many people might be interested in his model house gave Gordon the impetus to begin at once.

Gordon and Joyce have always shared hobbies and, at first, building a dolls' house seemed like just another one to share. Although Gordon built that first house, it was Joyce who fixed the slates on to the roof and primed the paint on the window frames. They named the house Rossville and put it on display at a local charity event in Dorset in 1986. There it was seen by the editor of *International Dolls House News*, who was so enthusiastic that they were encouraged to

Above **Gordon and Joyce Rossiter** with a house for a customer in Germany. It has nine rooms with 14 sliding sash windows. The parquet flooring took 4,500 pieces of individually cut sycamore.

Right **Rosslea**, a Victorian-style house which Gordon made for Joyce.

exhibit at a specialist dolls' house and miniatures fair. A few houses and a few fairs later, they decided that early retirement as a way of life might be just a little tedious, and 'Rosscraft' was born.

They now make to commission, and although both Joyce and Gordon have won many prizes for photography, which is another shared hobby, it is usually Joyce who takes the pictures of houses that may be suitable for miniaturization, photographing their architectural detail from all angles.

While Joyce takes the photographs, Gordon just looks – as a builder, he is used to sizing up buildings by eye. 'There are four courses of brick to every foot,' he says, 'and drainpipes and gutters come in six-foot lengths.' He can quickly estimate the height and other dimensions of a house, although he always carries a ruler in his pocket to check precise measurements.

Each commission will pose slightly different problems and need additional research from books. Sometimes they are given an idea to work on, and produce alternative suggestions and sets of plans, and although they have a large collection of architectural design books at home, Joyce often heads for the library to check up on house styles from other regions.

A replica of a 14-room sea-captain's house meant reproducing glass-panelled doors and stained-glass windows, some with semicircular heads which Gordon steam-bent in Joyce's pressure

important feature. At the 1989 Woodworker Show he won a gold medal for his oak elliptical staircase, designed as the centrepiece of a Georgian-style house for Joyce. So far the house has not been made, even though Joyce has some of the furniture ready and has planned out the interior decoration.

Gordon also devotes great care and attention to sliding sash windows – they have to be precisely fitted in order to work like the Georgian or Victorian originals. Period fireplaces, too, must be exactly right, and if the original fireplaces are missing from a house which is to be miniaturized they go back to their reference books. A visitor to a miniatures fair once suggested to Joyce that the bond of the brickwork on a fireplace in one of their cottage interiors was incorrect, as it was Flemish bond, and not English. In fact, they had been asked to base their model on the existing house, as it is now, which had been damaged in the last war and had a reproduction fireplace. Although Gordon could hardly recommend lighting real fires, it might almost be possible because, exceptionally for a dolls' house, his beautifully made chimneys are often fitted with two or even three open flues. The chimneys are made of mahogany with turned pots.

Living in Dorset, Gordon and Joyce are surrounded by picturesque thatched cottages, and they have made a number to commission. The thatching looks exactly like full-size combed wheat reed thatch, with a neat, close-cropped finish, which is not surprising, as they follow the same procedure as that used by the local thatchers. The only difference is that they use brush fibre instead of reed, and glue replaces steel battens, or 'sways'. The labour is much the same, too: it takes the two of them, working together, almost the same amount of time as it would take for a master thatcher and his

cooker. Unless a customer specifies glass, Gordon prefers to use acetate, as he feels it is less vulnerable. To colour it, he uses a translucent dye which can be flooded on to either material.

The staircase for the sea-captain's house took over 100 hours to make, with curved handrail and open, cut, bracketed strings. After drawing his scale plans, Gordon often starts work on a house by making the staircase first, as he feels it is such an

Top left Gordon's prize-winning elliptical staircase.

Bottom left Part of the chimney and roof detail of Rossway, a six-room Georgian town house based on one in Dorchester, shows the meticulous attention to detail so typical of Gordon's woodwork. This house was awarded a gold medal at the 1990 Woodworker Show.

Above A beautifully thatched Dorset cottage.

boy to complete a roof – about two weeks minimum, doing a full working day, six days a week.

First, Gordon drills the plywood roof with equally spaced holes until it looks almost like pegboard. A small cluster of brush fibre is bent in half to form a 'yealm' – a sheath that, in scale, is about the thickness of a finger. The yealms are laid in courses starting at the bottom of the roof. While Gordon holds each yealm firmly in position, Joyce secures it with needle and strong thread, which she takes through twice to secure it firmly. They use thousands of yealms to complete one roof, and each course is glued as well as stitched for additional strength. Each time they break off at night, the glue on the last completed course dries and stiffens. The next morning the first course to be laid is extra hard work,

as it is difficult to get the needle through.

The top edge of each course has to be trimmed neatly to shape at a slight angle to lessen the bulk before adding the next course, which conceals the stitching below, as they work back and forth along the roof. Trimming might have been a real problem if Gordon and Joyce had not acquired a knowledge of farm implements through living in a semi-rural area. Gordon uses clippers that are normally used by farmers for cutting sheep's toenails, as these are the only ones that can cope with the stiff fibre. The roof is completed with a ridge pattern, neatly stitched and trimmed in the traditional pattern of the region.

They were quite pleased when they received a commission to make a replica of a modernized Dorset cottage where the thatched roof had been replaced with slates.

27

'A change is as good as a rest,' said Joyce, although she then had to make and fix all the slates. The slates are made from reclaimed material. One day at their local printers they noticed some large sheets of black packing board that had been left lying in a corner, and found out that these were discarded packaging for films. Realizing that these were just the right thickness and rigidity to make

perfect slates, Gordon and Joyce asked if they could have them, and when the printer later closed down they took them all away.

The sheets are given a base coat in a suitable colour, then painted with Sandtex to add texture. After that, Joyce 'plays around' with paint until she achieves the varied colour and shading needed for each particular house. Rather than work with a paintbrush, she uses an almost-dry toothbrush to give the graining and character which is so characteristic of real slate. The slates are marked out to size, and then cut with a small guillotine in one direction and a Stanley knife in the other. The guillotine cuts the straight edges, but the Stanley knife is used to cut the lower edges at a slight angle, bevelled in the same manner as on real Welsh slate. A large roof may have as many

as 4,000 slates, every one of them individually cut and fixed in place by Joyce.

A more urban style of commission was for a 1/12 scale model of a newly built shopping arcade in Chichester, Sussex, including six shops. For their exact replica, they found a novel way of directly copying the originals. They took a camera and a pair of steps, and photographed each shop fascia board. Gordon enlarged the photographs, printing some glossy and some matt, and used these enlargements, carefully trimmed, on the fronts of the miniature shops, finishing off the lettering with hand colouring. The floor looks exactly like real marble, and Gordon reveals that they used coloured Daler mounting board, accurately cut to make the shaped tiles needed for the design, and then sealed the completed floor with diluted PVA glue which gave it the sheen of real marble.

When they receive a commission from someone living far away, it is obviously more complicated to work out with their client just what can be included and how that will affect the price. They send samples of suggested woods, flooring materials – wood, stone, or whatever is appropriate – and make up small samples of parquet flooring. They are often asked to complete the interior decorations too, and the customer will be sent a selection of wallpapers to choose from, as well as colour samples of suitable paint finishes. Gordon says he always agrees the exact specification in detail before he starts work, just as he did when building a full-size house.

Far left The miniature shopping arcade. The six glass lighting globes were made by Leo Pilley.

Left Rossbeck, a large timber-framed Suffolk house.

Brian & Eileen Rumble

The Scottish–American Connection

Many Scots have emigrated to America, but not so many English people can have first gone to work in America and then settled in Scotland. Brian and Eileen Rumble seem to have reversed the more usual sequence in several ways. Brian is well known for both dolls' houses and furniture, but the furniture came first. And although he is English, his reputation is built on his unique dolls'

houses, based on Scottish originals, which include traditional built-in furniture.

Brian and Eileen met and married when both were teachers at a school in Berkshire – Brian's subject was handicrafts and Eileen's needlework. Their travels began when Brian was offered a year in New York State as an exchange teacher, and they both enjoyed the United States so much that eventually they went back for four years while Brian took his master's degree. They then moved to Colombus, Ohio, where Brian lectured on design technology and gained his doctorate. When Brian took up a lectureship at Dundee College of Technology, they finally settled down at Strawberrybank Cottage in the delightfully named Backmuir of Liff.

The first small shift in the direction of their ultimate career came via Eileen. She gave up full-time teaching when they went to the United States, and instead used her needlework skills to restore costumes for antique dolls in a private collection. Brian has always had a special interest in period furniture, and cabinetmaking was one of his subjects. While in the US they both spent time looking at museum collections of fine eighteenth- and nineteenth-century American furniture, and built up a collection of books on both British and American furniture. So when, in Scotland, Eileen came home full of enthusiasm after a talk on miniature furniture, given at the local branch of the Embroiderers' Guild, the scene was set for her to encourage Brian to try the miniature scale.

For his first reproduction in miniature, he chose an American Hepplewhite-style chair, and Eileen helped with the upholstery. Once the prototype was made, he took advice on scale and then entered a 1/12 scale version in a Scottish miniaturist competition, held in aid of the Save the Children Fund. Not only did he receive a diploma, but the chair was immediately bought by the Museum of Childhood in Edinburgh.

Despite this instant success, for a while miniatures remained just a hobby, with Brian choosing an eclectic mixture of pieces to reproduce. His furniture ranges from Jacobean to Victorian and, reflecting his travels, includes American Colonial designs and some that are uniquely Scottish, like the Orkney chair and a child's hooded cradle.

He first exhibited some of his work at Longleat in 1984, when a display of dolls' houses and miniatures was staged there as a visitor attraction. Scottish collectors were beginning to provide a local market, and by the time Brian took early retirement from teaching in 1986 he felt he had made a good start on a new career. Brian and Eileen chose the name Rudeigin Beag – Gaelic for 'something small' – and turned professional.

By this time Eileen was as much involved as Brian. She undertook the final polishing of all the furniture – using French polish for the eighteenth- and nineteenth-century pieces, but wax polish for oak. Her sewing and embroidery skills were already an essential part of the enterprise.

Eileen tackled the upholstery on their Martha Washington chair, and points out that there are peculiar difficulties in working around such delicate arms and legs. The stretchers presented a special problem, and after a few breakages while she was experimenting to find the best method, they decided that Brian should add the stretchers *after* she has finished the cover.

The original of this Hepplewhite-style chair was made in 1780 and is said to have belonged to Martha Washington, wife of George Washington. The chair is much lower in the seat than most Hepplewhite-style chairs, and Martha is known to have been very tiny. This chair has the slender lines, finely scooped arms and elegantly shaped back which are all noticeable features in American adaptations of Hepplewhite designs in the late eighteenth century.

For furniture styles where embroidery is a useful addition, such as the hangings and coverlet for the splendid Jacobean four-poster bed, Eileen includes traditional Scottish motifs in her design. She works on a fine cotton crepon with a slightly knobbed finish, using feather-stitch so that she can take in the hem almost invisibly, producing an exceptionally neat edge on both back and front.

Brian and Eileen enjoy combining their talents. An embroidery stand, made in mahogany like the original, can be fitted with work either in progress or completed. Eileen always works on a frame, using specially woven net of a kind that is more often used for mounting superfine fabrics for wedding dresses. She finds it superior for her purposes to more expensive silk gauze. She draws out her design on tracing paper and pins it behind the net. The traced outline shows through, so that she can follow her design – rather like a cartoon placed behind a weaving frame – with just enough space between to work without catching her needle in the tracing.

Her favourite craft is lacemaking, and this was the inspiration for the lace pillow mounted on an oak stand. Such stands vary in style in different parts of Britain and Brian based his folding stand on one used in the Midlands. The needle lace used for each piece displayed on the pillow is so fine that it takes between five and six hours to make the tiny length. The pin holes have to be so close together that when Eileen has started working the pattern, it is impossible for her to see between them. She works with entomological mounting pins, normally used for mounting butterflies and insects, which are long and exceptionally fine, so that she can fit in enough holes to work a complicated pattern. In addition, if the tension is not perfect – and with so many pins, and 18 bobbins in use,

this takes great skill – the lace will start to curve. Eileen finds that she can only keep up this level of concentration for a relatively short time and needs frequent breaks.

In the late eighteenth century there was a revival of both marquetry and parquetry designs for decorating furniture. The effect was achieved by making up a design as an ornamental veneer, which was then applied to another surface, and this is one of Brian's favourite types of work. He has always enjoyed the visual effect of combining differently coloured woods, such as sycamore, holly, cherry and maple, and he uses the technique to produce a dazzling array of the tilt-top tables that were so

dimensional appearance. After the veneers are cut and numbered on the reverse, each triangular piece is scorched along one edge in hot silver sand, to add a subtle effect of shading. The timing of this process is a skill learned through practice and patience, as too much scorching will cause the veneer pieces to shrink so that they will not fit together neatly when assembled. The body of the table is made in mahogany, but the top is made of 1/16in (1.5mm) birch-faced ply, which is back-veneered and edged with mahogany before the motif is glued on. The crossbanding around the edge is applied last so that it covers the edge veneer.

For large table tops and sideboards the mahogany veneer to cover the exposed ply surface is quartered. The joints of the

Left Jacobean oak four-poster bed with hand-embroidered hangings and coverlet incorporating traditional Scottish motifs.

Above A firescreen with lace horse and pillow with 1/12 scale Bucks point lace; the bobbins were made by David Provan. The firescreen has a beadwork shield.

Right An elegant sofa table *circa* 1790, in mahogany with an inlay design. The table has two drop leaves and is supported on lyre ends with castors.

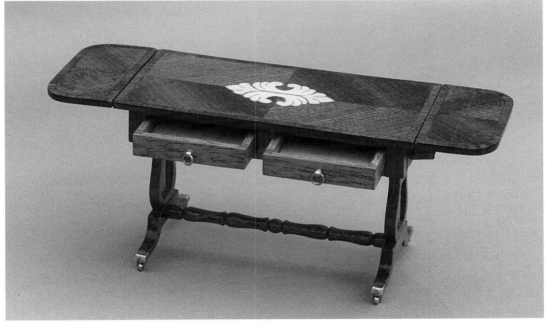

popular in smaller Georgian homes. He also uses motifs to decorate sideboards and sofa tables based on Hepplewhite designs.

Perhaps his favourite motif is the sunburst, which can be circular or oval, but is always spectacular. This design is particularly effective because of its three-

quartering align with each quadrant joint of the central design. Brian learned the hard way how even a tiny loss of concentration may ruin days of patient work. It was, predictably, when working up to the deadline of a miniaturists' show, that one evening he quartered the veneer for a

sideboard with the grain running in the wrong direction, and only realized this the next morning when the glue had set. As it was irremovably fixed in place he had to scrap the piece and make another complete sideboard.

Brian's customers soon started asking for dolls' houses, so that they could display their furniture in an appropriate setting. There were plenty of styles to choose from without going too far from home, as each region of Scotland has its own very individual houses based on the indigenous building materials available. Brian's first house was based on one in Fife, where the textured exterior rendering is known locally as 'harling'. Brian simulates this by covering the walls with industrial garnet paper, which is then painted white. The black paintwork and

black-painted 'corbie' (meaning crow) steps are striking features against the white of the harled finish.

Brian takes great trouble with every detail of each cottage: floors, doors, skirting boards and panelled wainscotting are all of oak. This first house won first prize in its class at the Royal Highland Show in Edinburgh, and in addition a Memorial Award for the most outstanding woodwork in the show.

In Aberdeenshire the local granite is a distinctive pink, so that his Aberdeenshire cottage, made to special commission, has a warm glow. This house became a big undertaking, involving the casting of around 1,200 slates and a large quantity of rubblestones, using moulds made from cold-set latex. He uses Plasticine to make his master originals and a variety of materials for the modelling. Das modelling compound produces good results for stone slates, which need to be thin but strong, while plaster of Paris or a Polyfilla mix works best for rubblestone. The stones and slates are painted individually in gouache to achieve variety of tone, and finished with a coat of matt varnish.

Brian is often tempted by special commissions and has tackled a Scottish manse, a Suffolk farmworker's cottage, and a house combined with village shop based on buildings in Fife, but with additional features incorporated to the customer's specification.

Brian enjoys providing traditional fittings in his cottages. One uniquely Scottish feature is a built-in box bed in the kitchen, with beneath it a 'hurley' – a drawer on wheels which was pulled out at night for the older children to sleep in. Above the bed there was also a shelf for the 'bairn'.

Brian and Eileen still have time for other interests – while Eileen is teaching lacemaking at evening classes, Brian is likely to be practising the bagpipes. He is now a member of the Blairgowrie Band, and when Brian plays, Eileen is able to take time off from miniature work and enjoy the music.

Opposite A Perthshire rubblestone cottage with dormer windows. Brian uses thin gauge pewter to simulate the lead flashings.

Opposite below A typical Aberdeenshire cottage in the local pink granite.

Left A traditional village house and shop based on an original in Fife, with the typical yellow–brown sandstone walls and roof hung with split stone slates.

Robert Stubbs
The Tudor Period

Many years ago Robert Stubbs visited Little Moreton Hall in Cheshire, the most decorative half-timbered house in England, with its leaded casement windows, white plasterwork and exuberant patterns of blackened wood. Robert never forgot his first sight of that incredible house, although he was already familiar with simpler half-timbered buildings from his childhood in a small village in North Staffordshire.

His father, as village carpenter, joiner and wheelwright, could make anything that might be needed by the farming community in which they lived, and Robert used to watch him at work. Almost everyone in the village went into farming when they left school, including Robert, although he subsequently went to agricultural college to gain a degree. Eventually he left the land to work as a technician in a Lancashire textile mill, gaining a second degree at night school,

this time in chemistry. Ten years after joining the company, Robert and a partner bought the mill, and ran it successfully until, in 1980, he decided it was time for a change.

By this time Robert and his wife, Renée, had six children to bring up. They each had three from earlier marriages, and wanted them to grow up away from the pressures of town life. They had had holidays in Norfolk for many years, and had come to love it, so Robert sold his share of the textile mill to enable them to move there, with the idea of starting something new.

Their home at Hopton-on-Sea is only 70 yards from the beach, and they first took over running the trampolines, then the beach shop, and then the sweet shop near the front. And then, suddenly, Robert developed the urge to do woodwork. He supposes that after spending his working life up to that time without giving it a thought, he must have inherited the ability from his father: he seemed to begin instinctively, without any conscious effort. He rented a workshop and advertised locally, offering to make furniture, and the orders came in.

Then one day the owner of the Model Village in Great Yarmouth called to ask if he would be willing to repair some of the model houses, all, as it happened, in 1/12 scale. Robert found it interesting putting right those houses that were in a bad state, and went on to make some new ones. It was very good practice for making dolls' houses, he says, but the only period which really attracted him was the Tudor of his childhood, and although he refurbished houses of a variety of styles and periods, the ones he made from scratch were all half-timbered.

The Model Village is a popular local attraction and word of Robert's Tudor houses soon got about. As a result he was asked to make one for a building society in Great Yarmouth, and it literally stopped the traffic. The building society displayed it in the window of their offices in the market place, which gets very crowded on market days. So many people stopped to admire the house that the traffic wardens politely requested the manager of the building society to put it inside rather than on display in the window.

It was while on holiday in London that Robert and Renée discovered 'The Dolls' House', London's first specialist shop, in Covent Garden market. Robert told the owner that he had made some dolls' houses, and she suggested that he bring one along to

Opposite
Robert Stubbs with a large Tudor mansion.

Left **Many-paned windows add to the dramatic effect created by this house.**

These houses have particular appeal in the United States.
 The gallery is an unusual feature.

he finds that he invariably sells a house almost as soon as each fair has opened. He sold one to the then editor of the *Home Miniaturist*, which gave him additional publicity, and soon received orders from the United States – black-and-white half-timbered houses really catch the American imagination.

Robert's houses are now in dolls' house museums in Britain and America, and even on show in Spain, and no two are ever the same. He has developed a real feeling for the period, and although he never draws detailed plans he thinks very carefully about the proportions, which are so crucial to success. The closest he gets to making a plan is to draw a rough sketch on a spare piece of wood in the workshop, and to work out the size of the base and the finished height of each floor. Robert wants to catch the flavour of the period, rather than to make an exact replica of any particular house.

The houses are built and finished one floor at a time. This way of working is uniquely suited to Tudor houses, with their overhanging jetties. He uses ⅜in (9mm) medium density fibreboard (MDF) for the carcase, and hardwoods for the beams and joinery. He likes to use parana pine if possible, because it is straight grained, hard, and carves well. Carving is something he always enjoys, shaping the beams so that they look ancient and worn. His favourite tool for this is one that belonged to his father, who adapted an old cut-throat razor by fitting the blade into a handle. Robert used the same tool for decorative carving on

show her, which he did on their next trip to London. She bought it and placed another order. Robert's Tudor houses seemed to sell well, but he continued to make his full-scale furniture. Then, while exhibiting at a show of the Guild of Norfolk Furniture Makers, he was shown a copy of *International Dolls' House News*, from which he learned about the miniatures fairs which were just beginning in England.

Robert found he enjoyed the fairs and the people at the fairs enjoyed his houses. Now

on to make a convincing lattice. Early Tudor houses were a bit short on glass panes, Robert mentioned, but real glass sparkles beautifully when the houses are lit up from inside. The lighting is concealed behind internal beams so that there are no anachronistic bulbs showing, and he uses 12-volt car bulbs which last a long time. The wiring is put in for each floor separately before final assembly, and he puts the transformer and switch or switches behind the back wall of the houses. Occasionally people will ask for separate switches so that each floor can be lit independently. He was once asked for 15-room house with separate lighting in each room, and says it looked like a telephone exchange at the back before it was tidied up.

Robert now always sells direct to the public, and attends up to 30 miniatures fairs a year. Some of them are two- or even three-day events, and although both he and Renée find the time at the fairs enjoyable, they take

his full-size dressers, to give them character.

His capacity for improvisation came in useful one Friday evening when he was finishing off a house to take to a fair at the weekend, and discovered he was running short of wood. He still had to add the second floor, and found he had enough for two bedrooms, but not an upper room between them, so he used the last piece of wood to construct a minstrel's gallery in the centre, based on one he had seen in an old inn – a feature which he now often includes.

The houses are painted using white masonry paint to represent the plaster infilling. Robert has occasionally decided to colour one Suffolk pink, or the traditional ochre that is sometimes used in country districts, but says that black-and-white remains the favourite with most of his customers. The roofs are a composition evolved as a result of experiment. An old kitchen fork, bent by design, not accident, is the perfect tool to mark out lines to simulate the texture of thatch, and the colour is produced with woodstain.

He uses standard ⅛in (4mm) window glass rather than acrylic for the windows, and the look of leaded panes is achieved by a precise mixture of paint and glue squeezed

Top **Carving beams is one of Robert's favourite activities.**

Above **Robert pays as much attention to interiors as exteriors, using panelling extensively.**

Right **A brick fireplace in a distinctively black-and-white room.**

Opposite **This house has brick infill, also characteristic of the Tudor period.**

up around 46 days a year out of his productive time in the workshop, so after a while he found he could not manage everything on his own.

Luckily he has a very large workspace, and over a period has gathered together a team of four helpers: Reg, Cliff, Mick and the youngest, another Robert. None of them were trained carpenters, although they all enjoyed woodwork as a hobby, but they have developed their skills through practice and example.

Each member of the team has his own way of working and takes a pride in incorporating his own special features. Although all the houses they complete are Stubbs' houses, based on Robert's initial ideas, the interior fittings vary. Such things as staircases, shelves and fireplaces, the way in which the beams are sited and jetties carved, are all distinctive hallmarks of the individual craftsman. Although there are two power saws in the workshop, most of the tools they use are hand tools. They enjoy a friendly rivalry, and say that when one of their houses is pictured in a magazine, they can tell instantly which one of them made it.

The first time I met Robert was in the middle of a busy miniatures fair in Surrey. He was standing by a house that took my breath away. The doors were wide open, showing the multiplicity of rooms which, in a real Tudor house would have been hidden from sight in a more random arrangement, but which, in his dolls' house, were planned out to give an overall view.

Robert is a happy man; he spends his days translating his deep feeling for the Tudor age into houses which make his customers happy, too. His houses are strongly built, so that their owners will be able to keep them to pass on – just as the owners of those first Tudor houses preserved their timber-framed homes for their descendants.

Bernardo.
Traettino
Italian Style

Bernardo Traettino came to England for a year initially, moving from the Rome offices of the Italian tourist organization CIT to their London offices. He started in the travel business as an interpreter, escorting tourists round Pompeii and then further afield in Europe and the Canary Islands. However, his stay in London was extended until he decided to remain permanently, and moved to an agency in the City of London specializing in business travel. This entailed him spending most of his time jetting around Europe making arrangements for major conferences.

Bernardo's business career provided him with the early financial stability that made it possible to begin on his next career – dolls' house making. This, too, was initially for a year. His first miniatures were pieces of dolls' house furniture made as a

Christmas present for a niece in Italy. Although it was his first attempt at woodwork since his schooldays, it turned out well and was much admired by friends, who suggested he ought to make some more.

Bernardo, pleased with his new hobby, obliged, and, as a result of his work being shown around, he agreed to make some pieces for both Heal's store in London and a toy shop in the King's Road with a special interest in miniatures. At this stage he aimed

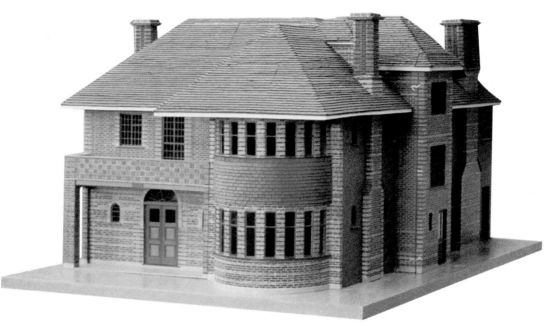

Above **A house modelled on one designed by Sir Edwin Lutyens, who also designed Queen Mary's dolls' house.**

Right **The beautiful patterning of the brickwork of the Lutyens house, faithfully rendered in paint by Bernardo.**

his furniture wanted to place an order. He found that he was enjoying himself so much that it was time for a sabbatical – to devote to his hobby. His plan was to take off one full year and then return to the travel business – but that never happened, because he decided to make a dolls' house, a field in which he excels.

In 1975 the dolls' house hobby in Britain had barely started, but Bernardo was aware that a few craftspeople were making miniature furniture to a very high standard, and that collectors seemed eager to buy. In those early days there were, however, few specialist dolls' house makers, so these beautiful pieces were displayed in very ordinary settings. He decided to try making a setting himself, but to a much higher standard than any he had seen. This would not just be a simple, front-opening house, but something more three-dimensional, with original ways of access. Unlike his furniture, and because of the initial motivation for this development, Bernardo's houses are always designed for adults. They are replicas of real buildings, produced to exacting specifications.

Bernardo based his first house on a sixteenth-century original in Broadway, one of the most beautiful villages in the Cotswolds. He started by taking accurate measurements and drawing detailed plans for the elevations and the interior, and spent a great deal of time working out exactly what he wanted to achieve. His care and thought resulted in an unusual dolls' house which

to produce really good quality dolls' house furniture for children to enjoy. His designs were simple, sturdy and carefully made, and thus of a higher quality than that generally available in toy shops at the time. Bernardo still makes this type of furniture, in both Georgian and modern styles, as he feels that children are now sometimes left out of the dolls' house hobby, which seems to have been almost completely taken over by adults.

At first he was able to pursue his new interest alongside his demanding job, but soon found that each shop owner who saw

sold almost immediately he took it to the King's Road shop.

Years later, at a party, Bernardo was introduced to a lady with the words, 'This is the man who made your dolls' house.' 'Oh,' she said, 'then perhaps you could come and mend the roof.' Bernardo not only repaired the roof, but the owner of the house is now his wife. They still have the Cotswold dolls' house that brought them together and which also, earlier, had been a turning point in Bernardo's own career. It is a remarkably accomplished house for a first attempt.

During his house-building career Bernardo has been asked to reproduce many period styles, from Tudor to twentieth century, but he still sticks to the guiding principles he worked out while making that first house. He uses the best quality plywood for the carcase, with solid mahogany for the facades – not for the beauty of the wood, but simply to provide a very smooth base for plasterwork. Window frames are made in mahogany with such precision that they can be painted and glazed before being fitted, whole and complete, into the window space. He uses $\frac{1}{30}$in (0.8mm) down to $\frac{1}{100}$in (0.3mm) thickness of glass, according to the scale required.

His houses are nearly always two rooms deep rather than the more common one-room depth of the usual dolls' house, with a view through to other rooms and perhaps a secondary staircase and corridors. He employs great ingenuity in working out a number of separate openings for access. For example, a section of the roof may lift up and it will be so neatly arranged that the join is almost invisible; a complete dormer may be hinged to lift up. Sections of the walls at the side will open separately or the centre front will swing open to reveal the hallway and staircase.

He does not cast mouldings – each one is made individually in wood. He wants the customer to have a completely hand-built

house where he as craftsman has made everything. He installs lighting in all his houses; if he feels electric light is not appropriate then he will provide concealed lighting instead, in order to reinforce the period feeling. In the larger houses there will be at least four or five separately switched circuits.

Work on a commission begins with a discussion of the budget and the particular features to emphasize. Sometimes the original house is too large to be copied in its entirety as it would take up too much space, so it may be decided to reproduce only the central part, leaving out service rooms and additional wings. When a house has to be adapted, he may provide as many as eight alternative designs showing the facade and a variety of possible room layouts.

Sometimes customers already have some special miniature furniture which they want to display, and in this case his room plans show the furniture drawn in to scale to help show it to advantage – for example, a harpsichord in a music room (*see* page 158).

When the finished design is chosen, he then makes a detailed series of plans showing the elevations, drawing in accurately every brick and slate in its final position on the exterior. Such detail is necessary because Bernardo uses the Italian technique of gesso work – plaster used as a ground for painting – to finish the exteriors of his houses. He scribes each individual brick or slate before the plaster sets. Finally he paints the plasterwork, faithfully copying the colour variations present on the original building. He finds it necessary to use various types of paint according to the finish needed.

All this expertise didn't come about without a few setbacks. Early in his career Bernardo tackled a replica of Gainsborough's house in Sudbury, Suffolk, which is now open to the public as a museum. As usual he took as many measurements as possible, but because it is a terraced house he could not

measure the depth on the exterior on either side. The staircase in this house is at the back, and after he had spent most of two weeks making and completing the staircase to fit in behind the main rooms, he discovered when he tried it in place that it extended beyond the outside walls at the back, as it was fractionally too deep for the space he had provided.

At first he was baffled and went back to check over the original house again. He then realized that because Gainsborough's house was Elizabethan, and had been given a new front in the Regency period, the untouched back wall was much thicker than on his plan, and took up more internal space than he had allowed. He had to alter the back of the house to put it right, and says this brought home to him how important it is to take every single measurement, both inside and outside – including even the thickness of each wall.

In another house his ingenuity was tested to the limit when he was asked to include a hidden priest's room. In the real house this

Top **This elaborate card model for a classical Rotunda demonstrates the immense amount of trouble Bernardo takes at the planning and design stage.**

Above **The interior of the Rotunda, which will be decorated with frescoes.**

was, of course, a secret room, its existence unguessed at by the casual visitor. It was barely more than a cupboard so that in 1/12 scale he had great difficulty in finishing the interior of this tiny room to the same high standard as the rest of the house. However, eventually the room was impeccably finished and the results are on view when a tiny bit of moulding is pressed on the panelling – and a hidden door swings open.

When living in Italy, Bernardo had plenty of opportunities to study the beautiful proportions of villas by Palladio. Since these had become his ideal, he was particularly delighted by a recent commission to build a miniature based on the Villa Capra – commonly known as the Villa Rotunda – his favourite among all Palladio's buildings. Originally built for both living and working, the ground floor of the villa had been used as a farm building, in a similar manner to the English hall house. The exterior and interior proportions are in perfect harmony, enhanced by the staircases symmetrically placed at all four corners –

which led to a major problem in the design of his model. How would the viewer see through to the frescoes in the domed, cylindrical central hall?

Bernardo's care in making a variety of accessible openings for his houses extends to thinking about the way in which they will be displayed – in a large or small room, in the open or against a wall, and whether the person looking at or into the house will be standing close by or sitting further away. He solved his problem by arranging that one whole corner, a quarter of the house, could slide out to reveal the interior and its frescoes. To make sure that the proportions follow Palladio's vision yet still work in the miniature scale, he made a 'maquette', a smaller mock-up in card and corrugated paper of the entire structure, together with the effect of his various proposed openings, so that he could study it from every possible angle before beginning work on his final, 1/12 scale version.

Also nearing completion is another house in the Palladian tradition of harmony and proportion – this time based on a house in Dover Street, London. Designed by John Nash in 1798 for his own occupation, it was eventually demolished in 1941 after war damage. Nash's grand design was for a very large house and the dolls' house version is based on the central section only, but even this has 15 rooms and two staircases. There are intriguing corridors and passageways connecting behind the main staircase, and the entrance hall will be floored in a tesselated design. For this, Bernardo will use real marble, despite the difficulties of cutting to scale and fitting. Following Italian tradition he prefers to use the exact material rather than to simulate.

In addition to all his practical work, Bernardo has always been active in promoting the work of British miniaturists and toymakers. As one of the first

professional dolls' house makers, he was invited to appear on the *Nationwide* television programme the evening before one of the first miniature fairs to be held in London, and as a result of this publicity the fair was packed.

He soon joined the British Toymakers' Guild, which had been set up in 1955, but he felt that not enough advertising was being done. He became chairman from 1979 to 1981 and again in 1988. Bernardo wanted the Guild to encourage wider public awareness of hand-crafted toys and miniatures, and instigated what has since become an annual show in London.

Since then the BTG has been so successful in achieving its aims that the fair is now attended by buyers from America and Japan as well as from many European countries. Bernardo always shows his work at this fair, although as a maker with an international reputation he no longer needs to advertise. But because of his long-standing connection with the BTG he feels a great personal involvement with the event, which is the only major show where the public have the opportunity to see the work of both toymakers and miniaturists side by side, and thus complements the many more specialist dolls' house and miniatures fairs.

Below The first Nash house, partly finished, showing staircase, designed and made by Bernardo for his wife.

Bottom Work is still continuing on the exterior of the stucco-fronted Nash house.

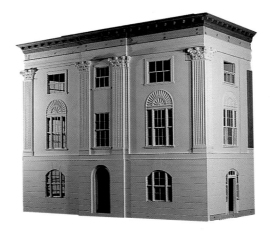

Trevor Webster
The Woodworker

When Trevor Webster left school he wanted a career that would employ his obvious talent for making things. There were two possible apprenticeships on offer: either to a cabinetmaker, which he felt he would really enjoy the most, or to a builder, with the prospect of learning management, which might offer better prospects in the long run. Practicality prevailed: he chose building.

However, you can sometimes get the best of both worlds, and while serving his building apprenticeship by day, Trevor also spent six years at evening classes in cabinetmaking, mastering the same skills he would have learned if this had been his full-time apprenticeship. Even so, Trevor worked for 30 years in the property business, until the development of an ear problem affecting his balance meant that he had to take early retirement. His two great interests, period houses and cabinetmaking, have at last merged.

While working in the building industry, Trevor had seen almost every type of period house from the inside out. He would draw room plans and study layouts, and work out the methods of the original builders. He became so familiar with different styles that he can now draw a plan of the room layout *inside* a house from just a thorough look at the outside, and he says he has never yet been caught out. As part of his job he also made many architectural models, which can be in 1/20, 1/50 or even, for a large project, 1/100 scale.

On seeing a mention of an exhibition of miniatures in a woodworking magazine, and thinking he was going to see some fine examples of miniature cabinet work, Trevor went along. The exhibition was 'Miniatura', and instead he discovered 1/12 scale dolls' houses.

By the time he himself exhibited, Trevor had seen dolls' houses by many other makers, and thought that there might be a gap in the market for something he knew he could make superbly – dolls' houses based

on period buildings. He did not want to paint or decorate, but simply to concentrate on the woodwork and bring out the architectural character of the original period, leaving his customers to complete the decoration to their own taste. As he saw it, his houses would become the wooden frames within which others could display their own fine collections of miniatures.

He did some market research and

Opposite **Trevor Webster with the Emporium, a late-eighteenth-century shop rather in the style of Fortnum & Mason's. There is plenty of living accommodation 'over the shop'.**

Above **Bayleaf – a Wealden house based on the fifteenth-century hall house at the Weald and Downland Open Air Museum at Singleton, West Sussex and, unusually for Trevor, made in 1/24 scale. He took 30 photographs of the hall house before he began work on his miniature.**

Below **Ever-appealing 1930s style in the Newstead.**

realized that he would need to make houses in several distinctive styles, and with different numbers of rooms, if he was to satisfy customers' varying needs. Before he started, he spent a lot of time thinking carefully about each house from the

which were to be prototypes for his first range of sizes, and when he took a stand at a miniatures fair they all sold straight away.

Trevor pointed out something that I knew instinctively but I had not understood why. 'If you are standing in a real room you

prospective decorator's point of view. He wanted to allow easy access, and also to make sure that the miniatures would be in rooms of proportions which would show them off to best advantage. Eventually, he set off with his camera, to photograph a variety of buildings in the neighbourhood, of which the proportions seemed ideal for miniaturization. He then made four houses

are looking at it from a height of, on average, 5ft 6in (1.67m),' he says, 'but someone looking into a dolls' house has an entirely different perspective.' He bears this in mind when scaling down, and has chosen nine inches as the perfect ceiling height for his dolls' house rooms. His room depth is never more than 15½in (39cm) otherwise there is not enough room for the decorator's elbow.

'It gets in the way,' he says. His windows are made with a deep rebate and he supplies the glazing separately, cut to size, so that it can easily be fitted into place by the customer after painting. He likes to install the wires for lighting behind his skirting boards, but if the

customer wants to deal with the lighting, he will leave skirtings unfixed, with a groove ready cut behind to enclose the wiring. His wife, Gill, helps out by identifying each piece on the reverse.

Staircases are made in sections, so that they can be removed to make decorating easy. Even in a four-storey house with mezzanine landings, each double flight can

be taken out and reassembled. Trevor's dolls' house version of 221B Baker Street, for a Sherlock Holmes enthusiast, is designed with the staircase at the side, as is customary in London terraced housing, but with separate side access – an interesting feature which meant that, as in the real house, room doors can be closed off from the stairway and landings. Trevor does not provide a plan so that people can put them back in the right sequence, and so far he hasn't been asked for one – which suggests that his designs do really work as he intends.

All the thought and careful planning that went into his first four houses paid off when he went on to adapt and extend these initial prototype plans. He could make not only a house one room wide but, where the architectural style was appropriate, a double-fronted version of the same house for a customer who might want something much larger. Wherever possible he gives his attic rooms dormer windows, and includes a lift-up roof. Used to working to tight budgets, Trevor makes sure he gives and gets value for money. The plans for each house are worked out with mathematical precision to avoid wasting materials: each is designed so that sections can be cut out of an 8ft x 4ft (2.5m x 1.2m) sheet of ply – the off-cut is only 1in (less than 3cm) in each case.

Trevor and Gill always attend miniatures fairs together, and both like to talk to the visitors and often take up their suggestions. It was as a result of talking to collectors that Trevor developed a range of period shops that had plenty of living accommodation. People would ask for a house with a shop on the ground floor more often than a small shop with just a flat above, he explains. Now he makes shops ranging from Georgian to Edwardian, which allow the collector room to expand. There are several rooms to arrange, as though occupied by an affluent shop owner, together with the shop itself, which can be used either for a specialist collection, or which can be used as an antique shop if the collector gets carried away and has too much furniture and too many accessories.

One original idea is a Victorian-style terrace with two houses and a corner shop, which is 37in (94cm) wide – still not too big for many dolls' house enthusiasts. Another unique feature which he can provide on his shops is a set of working blinds. For these, Trevor uses model ship chain and the pivots which fit into deck halliard pins of model yachts and has perfected a smoothly working mechanism. The material to use for the blinds seemed a problem at first, until Gill suggested using heat-reflective curtain lining, which has been treated so that it is stiff and does not fray.

Trevor has noticed some changes since he first started making dolls' houses in 1987. His customers are becoming more adventurous and seem to want larger houses, he says. In addition, there has been a growing interest in outbuildings and gardens. Any maker needs to keep up with current trends, and the result of his ear-to-the-ground policy has been the production of a variety of attractive small buildings for

the 1/12 scale gardener. He now also makes a stable block and conservatory as optional extras for the Oakham, his ten-room Georgian house.

A recent Georgian country house, the Vale, has a magnificent garden front with an impressive double entrance staircase, and a cleverly designed drop-front drawer which can be pulled out to make a garden table.

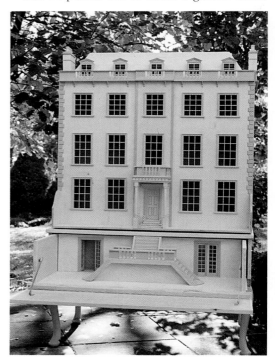

Right **The Vale, a Georgian country house with its own garden which can be folded away within the depth of the house.**

Opposite **The Granby – a late-Victorian bay terrace house** *circa* **1890, which is one of Trevor's most popular designs.**

This house can also be provided with its own stand, in the manner of the eighteenth-century 'baby' houses.

Like many other dolls' house makers, Trevor finds his Hegner saw invaluable, but he has adapted it by making a traverse table so that he can cut accurately, time and time again, window and door sections. He needs to make over 200 half-lap joints on the 19 windows for the Vale, for example, and he makes all his own architectural mouldings and floorboards. Trevor believes it is always worthwhile taking a fresh look at machine tools; so often with a fairly simple addition they can be made to do far more than the manufacturer claims.

Since he places so much emphasis on accuracy, I wondered whether anything had ever gone wrong. 'Yes, of course,' he said. But one mistake in particular still surprises him. 'I still don't know how it happened,' he told me, 'it must have been a memory lapse.' One day he put a roof on the Oakham, which has three dormer windows, and actually finished fixing it permanently in place before he suddenly realized that he was looking at blank plywood, with no windows – he had put the roof on back to front. He did manage to get if off without damage, but just a few hours later it would have been too late.

Trevor always enjoys working to special commission. It adds variety to his regular range of designs, and he will work out interiors to suit the number and size of rooms the client wants. The customer is always right, he believes – but with one reservation: he is not prepared to make a dolls' house which is architecturally inaccurate or which would not work in reality. The windows on his standard houses do not open, but he will make casements, provided the customer understands that the time this takes will increase the cost substantially.

Occasionally someone will commission a double-depth house, and this is something which really pleases Trevor, because he can then provide a staircase at a pitch which complies with current building regulations. In most dolls' houses, even his own, the staircase needs to be steeper than in a real house. Even so the maximum angle he will allow is 42°, which still looks realistic in 1/12 scale, rather than the too regular 45°, which is still so widely used.

Trevor is proud of his work and signs it – all his houses are stamped underneath with his name. They are built to last and he likes to think that in the future people will know who made them.

Ellie Yannas

The Artist

The dolls' houses made and decorated by Ellie Yannas are all illusion. Each one is an original work of art, demonstrating her considerable talent as a painter and her success as both designer and house builder. It was her interest in architecture that first led her to master basic woodwork so that she could make a simple dolls' house. She went on to improve on this until she now makes not only dolls' houses but has successfully marketed a variety of imaginative gift and packaging ideas based on architectural themes. Her imagination seems to be limited only by the time available to put her ideas into practice.

Ellie always knew that she would become an artist, and after taking a degree in fine art at Chelsea School of Art, she went on to exhibit her work in galleries in London and Brighton. At the same time, she masterminded the painting of full-size murals in Battersea under the auspices of the Greater London Council, who were keen to encourage groups of young people to improve some of the run-down parts of inner London.

Ellie enjoyed working with young people and her next venture was to design cardboard kits to make models based on vernacular Greek houses, which she thought would appeal to school-age children and demonstrate that these apparently simple houses were not all identical flat-roofed, one-storey buildings. These little houses were exhibited in the Bethnal Green Museum of Childhood and even went on sale in the Metropolitan Museum of Art shop in New York.

She made her first wooden dolls' house for her daughter, a replica of their own Victorian house in Battersea, and as at that time she was not constrained by any accepted standard, she chose 1/10 scale as being large enough for useful play. Ellie enjoyed painting the interior in facsimile of their own home, copying in miniature the decorative paint effects which she had originally done full size. In addition, she made a tiny version of the same dolls' house. 'I like the idea of a box, within a box, within a box,' she says, 'three houses one inside the other.'

Ellie's own preference is for classicism. She travels widely and on her first visit to Italy she saw Palladian villas which made a deep impression on her. This impression has been reinforced on each subsequent visit. After making that first Victorian dolls' house, she decided to create a miniature version of a Palladian building, but rather than an exact replica of one particular villa she wanted to use her imagination to the full. Both the

warm, glowing colours of the stonework and the painted interiors of the Italian Renaissance are ideal for miniaturization, and Ellie likes the idea of bringing together her different skills to make the perfect combination of architecture and painting. She found gouache the ideal medium to create the effects she wanted.

By this time she had discovered that the accepted scale for dolls' houses is 1/12. She exhibited her Palladian Folly at the London Dollshouse Festival, where her artistry made a strong impression but the villa did not sell. At that time the Georgian style was the most popular for dolls' houses. 'Perhaps collectors weren't ready for architectural follies,' she said. It was a simple, one-storey building on a stepped marble base, with a pillared, pedimented portico. The exterior was painted in glorious simulation of warm Italian stone. Inside, Ellie had created a fantastic and beautiful *trompe l'oeil* effect with marbled walls and tesselated floor, niches and statuary. It was unfurnished except for a Roman chair and a musical instrument left casually as though it had just been put down by a departing musician. The Renaissance feature of a central dome, which could be removed to give a bird's eye view of the interior, was also elaborately decorated.

Ellie also showed her Palladian Folly at the Chelsea Crafts Fair and then took it to California to show at the American version of the same fair, where it sold on the first day and led to further commissions. The dolls' house hobby had started several years earlier in the States, and people were already keen to try different styles. When she returned she found she had some more work to do.

Ellie's skills have also been used to great effect in the world of interior design and decoration. People from an interior decorating company who had seen the villa at the London Dollshouse Festival asked her to design a dolls' house with *trompe l'oeil*

decoration for them. It was to be used to display miniature versions of their distinctive, hand-painted furniture, which Ellie was also asked to make, and demonstrate the type of interior decoration which the company could carry out. She painted both exterior and interior features – windows, doors and even bookcases and curtains – and the walls of the large kitchen were decorated with a mural simulating green plants climbing up a garden trellis. As soon as it was completed, that house went on show at the Decorex Exhibition in London, which led to another prestigious commission.

Laura Ashley, having seen her work at Decorex, asked Ellie to make miniature versions of their contemporary range of furniture and fabrics for an eye-catching display. The furniture again featured the painted decoration which has since become so popular, and to miniaturize their fabric designs, Ellie hand-painted each one on to plain material.

It might have seemed as though Ellie had been lured away from dolls' houses to the world of interior design and decoration, but, typically, she managed to do three things at once. One commission she enjoyed was a relatively modern dolls' house, a very handsome one with a Queen Anne-style facade. The original is in St John's Wood, London, and was designed in the 1920s at the height of the Queen Anne revival by the then president of the Royal Institute of British Architects.

It was only recently that Ellie discovered the English Cotswolds, and realized that it is not only in Italy that stone glows with a sunlit warmth. Bourton House, at Bourton-on-the-Hill in Gloucestershire, a sixteenth-century manor house built in the lovely, yellow-tinted Cotswold stone, is a beautiful building and Ellie was delighted to be asked to make a replica as a dolls' house. The

Opposite **The brick-built house in Queen Anne-style: the brick facade is simulated in paint. The balcony was made for the house by John Watkins** *(see page 60).*

Right **Gilston House**, a typical house on the fringes of Chelsea and South Kensington, London. Ellie's model is so realistic that the only clue to its miniature size is the nameplate underneath.

Below **The library from Gilston House** decorated in the style of the 1980s, showing the fashion for painted decoration which has led to a revival of interest in *faux* painting.

Opposite **The Aviary** is fully 8ft (3.25m) tall.

manor house is large, and Ellie has designed the dolls' house in three separate sections which can be put together seamlessly so that it can be transported more easily.

She was asked to reproduce the interior as it is now, 'to capture a moment in time'. One part of the house is very much a home for the family today, while the rooms designed for grand entertaining by their ancestors in an earlier period are formal and magnificent. Ellie has provided exquisite painted decoration to show these two differing styles in her dolls' house. Details such as the reflection of sunlight on a wall, where it would fall naturally from a window, are painted in to give a lovely effect.

To be able to clearly see and reach the surfaces she is working on, most of this painting has to be done before the interior walls are fixed in place, and the first time she tried this technique, she spent hours painting dappled sunlight on a staircase landing, only to find that once the house was assembled it was never seen again.

When is a dolls' house not a dolls' house?

Perhaps the Aviary, completed in 1993, provides an answer to this riddle. 'It is a house for birds,' she told me. This is the most difficult and also the most exciting 1/12 scale house Ellie has made so far. The design is based on a staircase in Venice at the Palazzo Contarini, nicknamed the Scala del Bovob – the Staircase of the Snail – because it spirals like a snail shell. It needed to be strong and rigid and yet look light and airy, dreamy and mysterious, a true Renaissance setting for the live canaries which now inhabit it.

This project took 18 months to complete. Ellie found she needed to make a series of elaborate plans and drawings, followed by six months' concentrated work on the building, which was built piece by piece in the same way as the original must have been, before the exquisite painted decoration was finally added. There are 109 archways and 134 columns, all handcarved in wood. The capitals were cast in resin.

Perhaps the Aviary has no place in a dolls' house book – but it is a miniature home, a model of an extraordinary building in 1/12 scale –and it is to be lived in, although not by dolls. It also demonstrates the artist's creative intention, which is that anyone looking into this building must feel part of another world – that of Renaissance Italy.

When she left art school, Ellie intended to become a gallery artist, painting flat canvases. But she has an extra gift: the ability to create three-dimensional representations of buildings, painted in an extraordinary way that gives a magical impression of reality, an architectural fantasy. Buildings are the central theme of her work, and dolls' houses are only one facet of her many talents. She has designed an architectural letter rack and bookends for the Guggenheim Museum shop in New York. After that, in complete contrast, she intends to create a 1/12 scale version of the private theatre from the Palace of Versailles.

John Watkins

The Smith

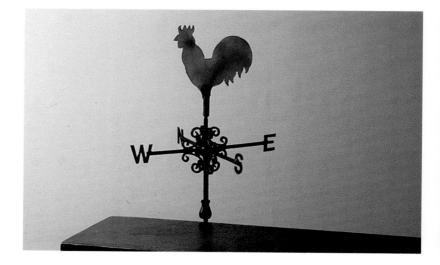

J ohn Watkins has established an international reputation for excellence in his specialized craft. Leading dolls' house makers such as Reg Miller, Mulvany & Rogers and Ellie Yannas commission him to make the architectural wrought ironwork they need to complete their finest houses (*see* pages 17, 18 and 57). Yet this is John's second career, begun only after he retired from teaching metalwork for 30 years in his native Wales.

John has always enjoyed his work. 'Metal is so tactile,' he says, and for the beginner learning his craft, it is a very forgiving material. With wood, if you slice off one tiny bit too much, the work may be spoiled, but with metal there are several processes to go through in shaping and forging, so you get more chances for refinement and, if necessary, correction, before you get to the final stage.

John bought his own anvil while still a teacher, ready for the day when he would be

Above **John Watkins working on a spiral staircase.**

Below **A miniature weather vane – the perfect finishing touch for a house or garden building – and yes, it does go round.**

able to set up his own forge, although this was not until many years later, when he retired from teaching. His intention then was to make wrought iron signs and hanging brackets for a local craft shop, but he was soon asked to make other items as well, including his first weathervane. However, one day he had an unusual request from a friend, a local estate agent. 'It would be nice, John, if you would make us a model to display in our window. It would attract a lot of attention.' A terrace of early Victorian town houses was being restored and converted into flats. A model of the exterior would show off the character of the buildings. John had never made a model house before, but the idea appealed to him, so he agreed.

He already had woodwork experience, which stood him in good stead in making the house, but he had to find a way of reproducing the architectural mouldings. He decided to carve a master and make a mould, then reproduce identical castings in resin for the corbels on either side of each window. This was successful, but that first house also had balconies and railings. Scaling down the metalwork presented new problems to be solved, but the result attracted all the attention expected by the estate agent, and more. The house was seen by the owner of a dolls' house shop and subsequently went on display there.

John was encouraged by her enthusiasm for his work to learn more about dolls' houses. She pointed out to him that no one was making miniature wrought ironwork, so he decided to make some more balconies and railings, this time in 1/12 scale, and exhibit them at a local dolls' house fair. This venture was a modest success. He sold all he had made at that first fair and

A wrought iron entrance gate which so enchanted a Japanese visitor to a miniatures fair that she bought it on the spot.

came home with just 10 pence profit: the hire of the stand was £10 and he made £10.10 from selling his small amount of stock. But John had by now seen a specialist dolls' house magazine, and realized that there would be plenty of opportunities for him to market his miniature work.

He had enjoyed his first experience as an exhibitor, so he booked stands at a number of other small dolls' house fairs, and at each tried to add one new design to his increasing repertoire. This led to his first special commission to make a balcony, railings and balusters to fit the staircase of a house made by a member of a miniaturist group.

In full-size historic architectural ironwork, both wrought and cast iron are sometimes used on the same piece. Similarly, if the exact repetition of a particular feature is needed in miniature work, some cast sections can be incorporated. John had learned to do traditional casting in aluminium at school, but now decided to try die-casting in a steel mould. He made a little chisel and carved out the shape he wanted to a depth of $\frac{1}{16}$in (1.5mm). He realized that white metal would be the most suitable material to use for miniature castings, and the only source of supply he could think of at that time was old car door handles, so he went to a scrapyard and came back with a carrier bag full.

To melt them down he improvised by holding them with tongs over the flame of an old paraffin blow lamp and allowed the molten metal to drip into a tin. To make the castings he remelted a small quantity, poured it on to the surface of his hand-carved mould and pressed it down with a block of wood. After some practice he found that this

the uprights, and ⅛in x ¹⁄₁₆in (3mm x 1.5mm) flat brass bar for the horizontal stringers. The stringers are drilled, and the uprights soldered in place. For a balcony, he uses heavier bar for the framework, first making a wooden base with holes drilled to take the uprights. He can then solder the decorative panels into the gaps. Since the delicate

method could be made to work but that he only achieved about one successful casting in seven – a good start, but wasteful of both time and effort. Now he uses low-melt metal alloy and a centrifugal casting machine, an expensive investment, but one which has proved invaluable.

To make simple railings he uses ¹⁄₁₆in (1.5mm) copper-coated steel welding rod for

castings could easily be melted by a soldering iron at the temperature normally used for electrical work, he uses a very low-temperature solder, and a light-dimmer switch wired into the circuit of his soldering iron means he can stop it getting too hot. Finally, the metal is given a first coat of primer and kept warm to accelerate the drying. He uses a few electric light bulbs as a

Opposite Differing styles of balcony on John's show house.

Left A spiral staircase finished in white looks elegant in a shop, house or conservatory. The staircase can be adjusted to fit different ceiling heights, and to rise either one storey or two.

Right John's Hampton Court gates in brass, before adding further detail and finishing in black.

Below John's masterpiece – the finished Hampton Court gates.

heat source, within an enclosed space. The final coat of paint is generally white gloss or black satin-finish car spray-paint.

On one occasion a particularly complicated balcony for a commission needed to be finished quickly. It included a lot of little cast panels which had to be soldered in place. In a hurry to get the balcony painted, he decided to try a quick-drying method – and put it in front of a domestic fan heater, forgetting that the solder used to fix the panels melts at 158°F (70°C). Predictably, it did all melt, and he then had to remake all the joints. 'Don't take short cuts,' he advises.

The handrail for a staircase is made from brass strip. To make it soft enough to work, this first has to be heated to a dull red, using a calor-gas blowpipe, then allowed to cool. It is then immersed in dilute sulphuric acid to descale it, and cleaned with wire wool under a running tap, polished on a rotating wheel, and then given a final polish with a rag and metal polish. A scroll end is made by John first filing the underside, so that it tapers almost to a point, then winding the scroll. John can also curve the whole rail so that, fitted to cast balusters and segmented steps, it completes a Victorian spiral staircase.

In 1983 John completed his most ambitious project, a 1/12 scale replica of the magnificent gates in the screen to the Fountains Garden at Hampton Court Palace, which were made by the great smith Jean Tijou in the reign of Queen Anne. John's tone is almost reverential when he talks about Tijou's work.

For all blacksmiths, wrought iron is the true medium for display, to work into scrolls and curves, tendrils and fronds. It is worked by flattening it out and folding it over, almost like making pastry, and the process is repeated again and again. If you look at very old, weathered wrought iron, you can see grooves, the result of this folding process,

which look almost like the grain in wood. It is the purest form of iron and its electrochemical properties make it far more resistant to weathering than cast iron.

The miniature Hampton Court gates are the result of three and a half months of concentrated work, often up to ten hours in a day. John got special permission to take numerous photographs from all angles and make detailed measurements. In his working drawings he had to allow for the different thicknesses of metal used in each of the sections he had measured, so that the miniature gates would look identical to the originals. His gates are made in brass. The largest uprights are square lengths of metal with the bottom end turned to a spigot to fit into the base board. As in the original gates, the cover strip (a flat length of metal which covers the gap where the two gates meet when they are closed) is riveted on, not soldered.

Most of the delicate leaf work, amazingly supported only by the stem at one end, is made from thin sheet brass which is tooled to reproduce the texture and fine detail of the originals. The unusual decorative feature of the *flambeaux* (flaming torches) presented another problem. Each has seven filaments (very thin wires) coming out of one stem, which in 1/12 scale becomes minute in size. After some experiment, John found that he needed to place his seven thin wires together inside a small copper tube, and squeeze the ends of the tube with a pair of pliers to flatten it. The wires then sprang out to give the desired effect. If you look closely you may detect some inaccuracies: John points out that these are copied exactly from those now present in the ancient originals.

The Hampton Court gates are the pinnacle of his achievement. 'I shall never make anything better,' he says. But already he is searching around, camera in hand, for inspiration for his next masterpiece.

Part Two
Furniture

David
Booth
Elegant Seating

David Booth's calm, quiet manner gives no indication of his real enthusiasms – until he spots an antique chair. Then his eyes light up and he rushes over to explore and explain the finer details, his hand resting lovingly along the curve of a scrolled arm or a hoopback: details come pouring out – when it was made, the type of wood, the care and skill which had gone into its making. He enthuses about the quality of the finishing, the patina of age and the delicate carving of a back splat, and turns the chair upside down to show the joints.

Although he makes a variety of eighteenth- and nineteenth-century miniature furniture, it is all related to the chair – firescreens to shield the face of someone sitting by the hearth, footstools and tables, dumb waiters to be placed conveniently so that people can eat in comfort. There are sofas and couches for the more indolent and, not least, that most enduring of styles, the Windsor chair in many of its regional variations.

David came to his speciality by a roundabout route. Born in the Weald, he still lives in Kent, in what used to be a picturesque village, complete with its own duckpond, but which is now an outer suburb of Folkestone, near the entrance to the Channel Tunnel.

When he was young he was uncertain what he wanted to do. He enjoyed working

shop, and as he also married the daughter of a grocer, it seemed natural to start his own business. David and Dulcie began with one grocery shop, found they were successful, and bought another. It was while they were running this expanding empire that David began to indulge his passion for antiques. He went to local furniture sales whenever he could, to look and learn, and spent his evenings studying books. *Country Life* magazine was an endless source of interest, as it showed pictures of rare and unusual

with his hands and started an apprenticeship as painter and decorator, then gave that up to become an apprentice fitter. He continued with this long enough to acquire basic skills in metalwork, and was offered a job servicing fruit machines. This also taught him more about mechanics and increased his improvisational skills. Even so, his career took off in a completely different direction before he could employ these skills in his own specialized craft.

David's grandparents owned a grocer's

pieces which he might not otherwise have seen, and he soon had a bulging file for reference.

His first opportunity to try his hand at antiques restoration came when a customer came into his store one day. The customer was on his way to the local antiques shop, carrying a Scottish corner chair which was missing a leg. David offered him £10, and the chair was his. He turned a leg on his father's lathe to replace the missing one, and at that moment discovered that what

69

he really wanted to do in life was restore furniture.

Gradually the loft filled up with old furniture that David intended to restore as soon as he had the time, and when the loft was full, more pieces would arrive and be left in the hall. Eventually some of the surplus had to go, but David did salvage a supply of beautifully seasoned wood to keep for future work, and much of this has since been used for miniatures. It is also supplemented with supplies from a local woodturner, who saves suitable off-cuts for David. However, there was to be yet another diversion before the wood was used for making miniatures.

Dulcie had begun making soft toys, and as they have always enjoyed doing things together, David became involved with this too, and he began making wooden toys to complement Dulcie's work. For both of them this turned into something more than a hobby. They began to exhibit at craft markets and were so successful that after a while they sold the grocery shops to concentrate on craft work full time.

David and Dulcie still enjoy working together, and the hand-polishing of all his furniture is something that they both find satisfying. Dulcie also tackles the upholstery and covers for the softer seating, where the main problem is in finding materials with small enough designs which are also flexible, and she often dyes her own fabrics and braid. Another difficulty is that however appropriate a fabric may look, it is only when she begins to work with it that she finds out whether it will drape and stretch as required. It always seems that she has only half a metre of the fabric which turns out to

be exactly right, while a two-metre length often has to be abandoned!

David began to attend woodworker shows, and bought a Como Turbo drill for which he made his own headstock and tailstock. His skew chisels are invaluable, but most of his favourite carving tools are old

Above **Different styles of Windsor chair in a variety of woods.**

Below **Two Regency chairs – a simple dining chair and a carver, both featuring ropework carving.**

ones which he has picked up in Maidstone market and ground down to his preferred shapes – something he still continues to do now that he makes miniatures. His first 'miniature' piece – in 1/4 scale – was, predictably, a chair.

Eventually he made his first 1/12 scale chair, a Windsor smoker's bow which won a gold medal at the London Woodworker Show. He went on to win gold medals at the

next two shows with first a lathback Windsor and then a hoopback, and after that concentrated entirely on 1/12 scale.

Windsor chairs are country chairs, developed during the eighteenth century from chairs made by woodturners, with one basic difference from more sophisticated, joiner's chairs – the laths and legs are mortised into the wooden seat, instead of the back edge of the seat being joined to a back support which continues to form the legs. The Windsor chair construction is very sturdy, and the wooden seats are gently contoured so that they are surprisingly comfortable.

The first Windsors were made of beech, but other woods – ash, yew or fruit woods – were soon used for more elegant versions, with curving bowbacks and pierced splats. For the miniatures, David likes to use a variety of woods, such as pear, apple, holly, lilac, walnut and mahogany, and although he mourned the loss of living trees during the

great gales in the late 1980s, he was compensated by the addition of some pagoda wood to his stock. Yew and ebony are favourites because of their fine grain, especially now that he is expanding his range to 1/24 scale; he says in the last few years customers keep asking for this size, so it is up to him to provide it. Looking at the minute size of the laths in the back of a 1/12 scale Windsor chair, I can only marvel at his rising to this new challenge.

David says that although he uses a magnifier, he mainly works by feel. His lathe

runs at 18,000rpm and the delicate spindles give the most trouble – they are $\frac{1}{16}$in (1.5mm) wide at the top, tapering to $\frac{1}{64}$in (0.4mm) at the bottom. The most important thing is to make absolutely sure that the grain of the wood is running straight through before beginning turning, as an infinitesmal bit off-true means that the spindle will break. He does burn his fingers a bit – 'used to it,' he says laconically – but finds that he can part off the spindles cleanly with no trouble. Turning is only part of his work; the hand-carved ropework on his Regency chairs and *chaise longue*, or the Victorian sofa, is an exceptional feature – and very time-consuming .

David has customers all over the world and takes great care that his furniture will not be damaged in hot or damp climates. He has worked out methods to ensure that table

tops, for example, do not warp. In full-size tables there is an allowance for movement, but this is much more of a problem in 1/12 scale, where the effect of any adaptation has to be almost invisible. Bowback Windsor chairs are especially vulnerable, as the bow could easily spring apart in some climatic conditions. If you look at one of David's chairs through a powerful magnifying glass, you will see an extra stiffener inserted into the curving back to prevent any such disaster – but how he does this is definitely the master's secret.

A finely made couch, with the sabre legs and bolster cushion typical of English Regency seating furniture.

John
Davenport
The Cabinetmaker

When John Davenport began helping his father to restore antique furniture 30 years ago, he quickly realized that he wanted to continue in this line of business. He would certainly have been very surprised to know that he would eventually become renowned for his superlative skill in making replicas in 1/12 scale of outstanding examples of the eighteenth- and early nineteenth-century cabinetmaker's art.

Sharing his father's love of fine furniture, it was natural for John to follow in his footsteps, complete an apprenticeship as a joiner and go into the family business.

Amongst the wide variety of furniture that was brought in for repair, there were occasionally small-scale pieces. John was immediately fascinated by these, which were collectable even then, although not yet reaching the high prices at auction that are now achieved for 'apprentice pieces'. (An apprentice piece is a small-scale cabinet or chest of drawers, made by a joiner or

cabinetmaker as a test piece to show his capabilities at the end of his apprenticeship. A genuine piece will be very well made and finished, with well-fitting, dovetailed drawers, handles precisely to scale, and the patina which only a beautifully finished piece of furniture acquires as it ages.)

There is also another category of superb small-scale work: the masterpiece. This would be made for a special exhibition, or as a test piece by a craftsman wanting to join a prestigious guild. John's work today meets the same criterion, and is as sought-after as the superlative examples of the past, many of which are now displayed in museums. There are few opportunities for today's miniatures specialists to make such pieces as a test of skill, rather than just for exhibition purposes, but John had to follow the same procedure in order to become a Fellow of the International Guild of Miniature Artisans, the American-based guild devoted exclusively to work in miniature.

As his interest in small scale grew, he began to attend as many sales as he could. He would have liked to acquire some of the

Opposite **John Davenport** in his workshop.

Left A German bureau cabinet in walnut, banded in satinwood.

French secretaire made in veneered amboyna burr, banded in kingwood, with working locks and marble top, and a beautifully fitted interior.

genuine eighteenth- and nineteenth-century miniatures, but already the market had begun to value the skill which had gone into their making, and he was always outbid. However, he did have the presence of mind to take measurements of anything he saw that he found exciting, so that he could make a copy.

His first contact with the dolls' house world came much later, when he restored a badly damaged dolls' house which arrived for repair. He enjoyed putting the house to rights, and decided to share a table with another craftsman at a dolls' house and miniatures fair. It was an interesting experience, because he wasn't really sure what to expect – miniatures fairs then covered a variety of things – dolls, toys, and both old and new miniature furniture.

John's wife, Julie, had always been keen on making things, and was already producing her own range of basic furniture intended for children's dolls' houses, so she took some along too. At that time 1/12 scale was not yet the international standard for dolls' house collectors, and John's furniture was larger, mainly in 1/6 scale. Julie did very well and sold all her inexpensive pieces, but for John the fair was not a success – there were no collectors at the fair to buy his perfectly finished work. However, it was a start. John changed to 1/12 scale, and with the swiftly growing number of miniature fairs and exhibitions he began to establish his reputation with serious collectors. He had plenty of wood to use, much of it from his father's workshop, and he is still using some of this fine-quality timber today. He cuts it into useful-sized pieces ready for use and stacks it for about three weeks. Given the age of the wood and the careful way it has been stored, it is safe to assume that it is not going to warp.

There are still problems to watch out for when the furniture he makes is bought by collectors in other countries, where there may be additional humidity. With a full-size cabinet, the thickness of wood used on the side pieces will probably be ¾in (19mm) and this is not very likely to warp. But when the thickness is only ⅟₁₆in (1.6mm) it is always a possibility, and John has to take precautions to ensure that it cannot happen. Certain woods are, of course, more prone to warping than others, and John's own favourite – for its stability, as well as the beautiful grain – is walnut. Provided care is taken in choosing a suitable grain size for the piece, he recommends walnut as an excellent wood for anyone thinking of making miniature furniture.

John feels very strongly that his miniatures should be made in exactly the same way as the eighteenth- or nineteenth-

century originals, and still spends most of his spare time studying fine furniture. English furniture in the early nineteenth century was influenced by French styles, as many French cabinetmakers fled to England at the time of the Revolution and began to work in London. He has miniaturized some exceptional pieces from that period, many of them showing a marked French influence. Occasionally he will eliminate some small detail, not because he cannot reproduce it, but because an over-abundance of ornamentation can swamp a piece which may measure only 5½in (13.8cm) in height.

He never changes the method of construction, always using the same types of joints as in the originals. Carcases are made of oak and then veneered; legs in all their variety are handcarved. One feature he particularly enjoys is an elaborate pediment, on a cabinet or secretaire-bookcase, handcarved in the round in the same way as those made in the time of George I. Although the back is never seen in all its detail on a full-size piece, he dislikes the practice of carving the pediment merely on the front, which destroys the integrity of the piece. He relishes the fact that the collector will be able to turn his piece to see it from all angles. He also attaches great importance to making exact facsimiles of working locks, escutcheon plates and keys. When he began miniature work, he spent months in his workshop experimenting and learning how to construct them, as he had no formal training in metalwork.

To John, the cleaning up and finishing processes are paramount, as no matter how good the workmanship, any miniature can be ruined in these final stages. His golden rule is 'never hurry'. He drills handle holes before he begins sanding with garnet paper grade 5/0 and 7/0; for the final finish he recommends silicon carbide 'wet and dry' Lubrasil 165. He says he cannot emphasize too strongly that care in handling is

Above A French commode with kingwood crossbandings and marble top.

Below A mini secretary, made in walnut with working drawers, in 1/50 scale.

essential during finishing – it is all too easy to snap a leg which at the base may taper to $\frac{3}{32}$in (2.5mm). He checks with a magnifier that the piece is sanded to perfect smoothness before wiping it carefully with a dry cloth, and then with a piece of cotton wool moistened with methylated spirits. He never uses clear filler because it will show up as lighter than the wood when dry, but prefers a walnut- or mahogany-tinted filler where appropriate. To achieve a soft look with the same degree of patina as that on the piece he has copied, he generally dulls the work, using grade 0000 steel wool before wax polishing.

John is a neat worker and his workshop is tidy. He always follows the same routine when he is making a piece, putting each part on a tray as it is completed, so that nothing will get lost – some of the parts are exceptionally small and could easily be lost on a crowded workbench. He recalls the evening that he put his tray on a shelf, with all the pieces ready to assemble the next day, and during the night heavy rain found its way through the workshop roof and dripped into the tray. The next morning John found all the veneered pieces floating in water, completely ruined. But the really sad thing was that the leak had been directly over the

Opposite **The miniature baby house: 7in (18cm) high, made of oak, veneered in burr walnut. The marquetry is holly, and the cabinet has working locks. The finely detailed interior was fitted out by Jim Martyn.**

Left **The exterior of the baby house cabinet. A superb example of the miniaturist's craftsmanship.**

tray and nowhere else in the workshop. With the quiet determination which is so typical of him, John started again as if nothing had happened.

Most of his work is commissioned these days, but not all – sometimes he cannot resist making a model if he sees a piece he really admires. He enjoys variety, and each year makes a few pieces in 1/50 scale 'just for a change'.

Another original idea has become a strictly limited series, to commission only. When he was shown some photographs of the beautiful eighteenth-century cabinet decorated and furnished by Sara Ploos Van Amstel (now in the Gemeente Museum, The Hague) John thought of making a 1/12 scale cabinet suitable for use as a miniature 'baby' house.

He realized that he could not fit out the entire cabinet himself, as well as keeping up with all his other work, and invited Jim Martyn, who revels in extremely small detail, to collaborate with him on this project. Jim is responsible for all the interior decoration and 1/144 scale furnishings of each cabinet, and they have now completed four in this very special limited edition. Each eighteenth-century-style cabinet house is unique, and has proved a satisfying, as well as a time-consuming, project for the two miniaturists.

Josie & Danny
Drinkwater
Upholstered Furniture

Above Josie and Danny Drinkwater with their dolls' house, which has eight rooms and a fine staircase. The Georgian doorcase is not unlike the one on their own house. The house is an eye-catcher on the large landing of their home, and makes an ideal showcase for the miniature furniture.

Right An X-framed stool with turned stretcher and a fender stool, both covered with handmade needlepoint worked at 28 stitches to the inch. Josie designs all her own needlepoint; she uses a magnifier to work and finds it a relaxing change from woodwork and upholstery.

Tetbury is a sleepy Gloucestershire market town with a mixture of medieval and Georgian houses. The enormous church, like many in the Cotswolds, owes its size, to a great extent, to the fortunes made by the local wool merchants. Just round the corner from the market house, with its Tuscan columns and ancient, sloping floors, is the home of Josie and Danny Drinkwater.

Tetbury Miniatures began with a dolls' house – or at least, the plan for one. Until he retired, Danny had been head of art at a Tetbury school. Not one to sit about, he turned his carpentry skills to restoring full-size antique furniture, and still found he had more time than before to devote to his hobby of woodturning. Josie suggested that he might make her a dolls' house, which she could furnish herself, and when he agreed, she decided to make a start on the

furniture at once.

Right from the start it had been her idea to make miniature versions of upholstered furniture, which in full size was already one of her specialities. She taught needlework and craft subjects at the same school as Danny, until she retired the year after him, but had always been interested in period furniture. She had reupholstered some of their own antique chairs, and when their children were small did some work from home, obtaining commissions through a local antiques shop.

Josie was so delighted with the idea of trying out miniature scale upholstery that she had rather pushed to the back of her mind the fact that first she would need to make the furniture, but now set to with a will. There was plenty of well-seasoned wood in Danny's workshop, and she asked him to find her a piece that would be suitable for her first attempt. Starting ambitiously, she decided upon a dining table and a set of chairs, for which she could supply the upholstered seats, covered with *petit point*. She began with the table, which she thought might not be too difficult for a beginner. She cut the basic shapes with Danny's band saw, and soon realized that carving the detail by hand with a craft knife would make heavy weather of what might have been an enjoyable task. Danny agreed, so they bought some proper tools – a Hegner fretsaw and Minicraft drill with a variety of carving heads. Josie found she liked working with power tools and after

A three-seat centre sofa, buttoned and fringed, ideal for conversation.

that there was no stopping her, although in those early days it was a great help that Danny was around to offer advice and assistance. It was clear that having the right tools was absolutely essential: it has enabled them to develop the wide range of furniture which they now produce together. In addition to the Hegner, Danny acquired a planer–thicknesser, which means that he can plane the wood for the miniature furniture accurately to a thickness of $\frac{1}{16}$in (1.5mm).

More recently, Josie has acquired a dentist's burr to use for carving. The great advantage of this is that she does not have to hold a drill, which can begin to feel very heavy after she has carved 48 legs for sets of chairs. Although she is not really into mass production, Josie does like to make one part at a time: legs one day and arms the next.

After making the dining room furniture for her promised dolls' house and completing the needlepoint chair seats, Josie saw a wing chair in a local antiques shop which she thought would be just right for her first attempt at an upholstered chair. To supplement her hands-on knowledge of present-day upholstery she looked into the methods used in different periods – it is important to go back to source if she is to make her miniatures in the same way as the originals. One way of doing this was to go to period houses that are open to the public, purely to study the furniture.

Following the original methods of construction, Josie's upholstered furniture

has a frame made with slots for securing the material to the inside of it. The reason that so many home-made period dolls' house chairs look amateurish, she told me, is because the padding and cover are just glued on. In contrast, on her wing chair the fabric is rolled over the arms and taken down inside, where it is fastened into the frame.

In addition to the more elegant eighteenth-century furniture, where the wood and its covering are designed to complement each other, she enjoys reproducing mid- and late-Victorian 'over-stuffed' chairs and sofas. The Victorians considered comfort to be more important than aesthetics – and Josie's accurate copies certainly look cosy. Suitable materials and trimmings can be a problem, although she has made some lucky finds in local markets.

When Danny retired from teaching he began work on the full-size four-poster bed which he had looked forward to making as soon as he had the time – and time he needed: because of his other interest in restoring antique furniture, the bed took him

essential. Even then, making frills that do not stick out at odd angles is an art which takes practice and patience.

It was really that bed that made them decide to exhibit at a miniatures fair. Josie decided to make a 1/12 scale version, and enjoyed making the bed and its hangings so much that she got carried away and made five more. While planning Josie's dolls' house, they had visited some miniatures fairs and specialist shops and now, as that was

Opposite **A fine four-poster bed with delicate lace-edged hangings. Josie buys some of the fine silks she uses for covers and hangings from an Indian sari shop. The delicate fabrics are exactly the weight and texture she prefers.**

Left **The Knole sofa looks very inviting; Josie provides cushion squabs which look faintly sat on without being in the least untidy. The neat finish is reinforced by the minute piping on each cushion.**

three years to complete. When, at last, it was finished, Josie made the hangings and coverlet. That bed was the inspiration for the dolls' house-size four-poster beds which have since become Tetbury Miniatures' trademark, and which give Josie the opportunity to make lace-edged sheets and pillowcases, and a frilled canopy and hangings. Making such things in 1/12 scale is a skilled craft, as one of the hardest things to achieve is flounces and valances that hang correctly. The thinnest materials and trimmings and the tiniest stitches are

still unfinished, Danny suggested that perhaps they had better start selling miniatures before their home overflowed with Josie's 1/12 scale furniture. So she put her prototypes in a glass-fronted cabinet, and Danny agreed to start making the turned elements so that Josie could concentrate on new items, the upholstery and fine needlework.

One new model is a Knole sofa, reproducing one of the earliest examples of upholstered seating, when for the first time the joiner and the upholder (upholsterer)

collaborated to try to produce something comfortable. The famous original sofa (still to be seen in Knole, in Kent) was much copied at the time and the design is still popular today. Josie's miniature is based on a Victorian reproduction from a friend's home, which has a major advantage over the original sofa. Early pieces often included imperfectly cleaned animal wool, which smelled strongly, an effect which got worse with time. By the nineteenth century the more fragrant and hard-wearing horsehair was used instead. Josie makes a solid wood base for the sofa so that it not only looks correct but also feels right. The firm structure adds to its authentic look, she says (*see* page 157).

As they got busier, Danny also took over the making of the beds, with their turned posts. He still uses the same lathe to turn the 7in (18cm) bedposts as he employed for the 7ft (2.1m) tall posts for their own bed. Like many other miniaturists he likes to use full-size machine tools, as they will suit any purpose: you can do very small turning on a large lathe, but you cannot do large turning on a miniature one, he explains, and he does not want to fill up the workshop with too many machines.

Living in Gloucestershire, Josie and Danny have never had any problem in finding suitable wood for their miniatures, particularly since the gales which have felled so many trees in recent years. While they may not need enormous quantities, they do want to be able to select for quality and variety and, in fact, are often given whole trees by friends. In true neighbourly fashion, they try to make something in return for the gifts of trees, and Danny recently turned a set of lace bobbins for a friend who specializes in this craft. Fortunately they have an ample supply of old walnut, which is the perfect colour and grain for beds and chair frames. This has been cannibalized from three

wardrobes, which all belonged to the family.

Josie and Danny both seem amused by their version of a doctor's couch, which they were asked to make by a persistent customer who was sure they could supply one. 'No,' they told her, 'we don't work in leather'. But the collector knew what she wanted, and even sent them some pictures, so eventually they agreed, as a one-off. However, as sometimes happens (*see* page 111), when they displayed it on their stand at a miniatures fair, ready for the customer to collect, they took several further orders which they could hardly refuse.

Their latest idea was sparked off by overhearing two collectors discussing how they were going to furnish their dolls' house attics. 'It would be such fun,' she says, 'to make a range of very old-looking, distressed furniture. I would love to make a *chaise longue* with the springs hanging out.' One problem might be in finding suitable shabby material for the ripped covering, although she is working on that. She has already found a source of suitably sized springs: pump-action dispensers for liquid soap or hand-cream all contain a tiny spring and to get at it, all she has to do is remove the plunger.

Both Josie and Danny still seem faintly surprised that they are making and selling dolls' house furniture professionally. When Josie first suggested the dolls' house, her idea was just to furnish it for herself – she didn't envisage making such complicated wooden pieces, and certainly not in quantity. Danny, too, never had any intention of becoming involved beyond the dolls' house, which he has at last finished. They seem to be the ideal partnership; their skills complement each other as they discuss and develop new ideas and become ever more enthusiastic about miniature-making. They clearly both enjoy what they are doing and get a great sense of achievement from working out solutions to each new problem.

Top left A Swedish-style sofa made in yew wood which makes a good contrast with the dark-green velvet cover.

Bottom left A comfortable-looking Victorian double-arm sofa with a carved back, and pretty toning cushions.

Barry Hipwell
The Innovator

Barry Hipwell is a man of wide-ranging interests. He speaks French, German and Japanese (the latter not fluently, as he hastens to say). He paints and sculpts, using a variety of materials. He has also trained as a singer and has enjoyed singing in opera – as well as constructing sets for the theatre. At one time he made jewellery in Soho, then later worked as an aeronautical model maker. Perhaps most surprisingly of all, he appeared for a while as a dance-mime with a Japanese theatre company performing in Paris.

Most of these fragmentary careers opened up almost accidentally, through some chance meeting or recommendation. Things happen to Barry often enough, it seems, for him to pick and choose, but in the last few years he seems to have found his *métier* as one of Britain's leading makers of miniature furniture. Even here he doesn't make furniture from just one period but, as he puts it, he specializes in not specializing.

He actually began as a tinsmith, working in the family firm, which made cooking utensils to supply to traditional ironmongers, so any form of metalwork comes naturally to him. This skill was refined further when he began designing and making gold and silver jewellery.

Barry's workshop is one of the smallest I have ever seen and in it he has an unusual assortment of tools. Crammed in are all the remaining tools from the tinsmith business, as well as his tools for jewellery-making. It was a long time before he settled down for long enough to concentrate on their use, but some of his other experiences have also contributed to his most recent choice of career.

Barry originally set his sights on the theatre, took voice-training lessons and joined the local choral and operatic society. He moved into a different branch of theatrical work when he was asked if he would like to join the Mermaid Theatre Company as a stage carpenter. At that point, Barry knew nothing about carpentry, but he did want to live in London, so he jumped at the opportunity, and stayed with the company for six years. By the end, he had developed both skills and imagination in his woodwork.

In London, Barry could visit museums and art galleries which stimulated his interest in craftsmanship, and also generated an enthusiasm for Japanese art which has endured ever since. It was at this stage that he switched from building theatre sets to designing and making jewellery, but this in turn came to an abrupt end when he met a Japanese percussionist who was performing in a dance and mime show, and had the chance of joining the company for their next

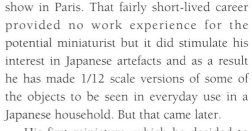

Opposite top
Barry Hipwell carving with a gouge of his own making.

Opposite below
A Swiss Fribourg *armoire, circa* 1815.

Below A strongbox dating from around 1500, probably South German. The miniature is made in mild steel.

show in Paris. That fairly short-lived career provided no work experience for the potential miniaturist but it did stimulate his interest in Japanese artefacts and as a result he has made 1/12 scale versions of some of the objects to be seen in everyday use in a Japanese household. But that came later.

His first miniature, which he decided to make one day for no particular reason, was a Regency card table, based on one he owns. He enjoyed the work, the little table turned out well, and he decided to exhibit, and, he hoped, sell his work at a local craft fair. To his disappointment he found that 1/12 scale, which he had chosen 'because it just seemed right', was unsuitable for the craft market and he was advised to find a miniatures fair.

He worked very hard to produce a variety of furniture so that he could see which types appealed to potential customers. Some of it didn't sell at all, he said, possibly because other miniaturists were already filling the demand for particular periods. He had begun with Regency chairs – based on Thomas Hope originals which he thought quite extraordinary – but these did not find a ready market. However, his Tudor tables, chests and joint stools sold out. Tudors seemed to be in demand so he decided to concentrate on that period.

His first major piece was a sixteenth-century Nonsuch chest, based on one he had seen in Blakesley Hall, Birmingham. The original is exceptionally large, over 6ft (1.8m) in length, and Barry used more than 6,000 pieces of inlay in making up the marquetry design, so it was a major undertaking. He has since made several examples of this, and on one occasion came to grief when a lid warped after its veneer was added, and would not fit. He had to

85

The cabinet Barry copied from the one in Fairfax House, York.

make another, but followed historical precedent in using the misfit as a table top, where it could be firmly fixed down. Panels from old chests are known to have been reused in this way, he told me, which is one

of the reasons that there are now so few complete Nonsuch chests to be found.

Barry does his research very thoroughly; he loves to visit museums and look at old furniture. A trip to a Leicester museum resulted in a replica of a German iron strong box with a working lock. The original was handsomely engraved with two figures and foliage, and on the miniature these are etched to give the same effect in the smaller scale. Barry found he needed to do further research in order to produce the authentic lock, which shot a set of bolts simultaneously

with a single turn, and spent a profitable day at the Lock Museum in Willenhall. He told me that this fascinating museum includes both the house and workshops of a Victorian lockmaker, complete with his tools and remaining stock, which is complemented by a collection of historic locks.

Barry has perhaps become best known for his inlaid and veneered furniture from the William and Mary period, and this is now his current enthusiasm. When he saw a magnificent early-eighteenth-century cabinet-on-stand, featured on *The Antiques Road Show*, he says he really got excited. The cabinet was not a 'find' but had been loaned for the programme from Fairfax House by the York Civic Trust, because it was such a superlative example of its type.

Barry wrote to the curator and, after permission was obtained, he was able to visit to photograph and take measurements to scale down for his miniature. The challenge to him was to reproduce the exquisite marquetry cartouches with flowers inlaid into the spandrels, and to make 48 compartments and pigeon holes which included 23 drawers, 21 of which were intended to be kept secret. Barry, inventive as ever, decided to put in a few extra drawers, and his miniature contains 36.

While in Fairfax House, which contains an exceptional collection of fine furniture of the period, Barry saw another chest-on-chest which he found equally inspiring, made in 1690 in kingwood (a type of Brazilian rosewood). He is waiting until he finds some kingwood with just the right figuring so that he can reproduce the spectacular orange and golden-brown colouring with a hint of violet. This cabinet features the oyster-cut veneering which was often used on furniture of this period. Oyster-cut is a section taken across a branch rather than the more usual lengthways, and for some pieces Barry cuts from twigs of walnut or yew. Make a friend of your local tree surgeon if you want unusual wood to make miniatures, is his advice. He rang round all the tree surgeons in his area initially, and one now saves him anything interesting from the trees he has cut down or lopped.

Both Tudor and William and Mary furniture include ivory in the inlaid designs, and at first Barry found it impossible to achieve the green staining needed to give it a leaf colouring in a marquetry flower design. He tracked down the author of a book on ivory carving who was able to advise him, and now uses a mixture of verdigris and vinegar. The acetic acid of vinegar is just strong enough to bite into the surface of the ivory, allowing the green copper oxide to be deposited, but Barry says it took a lot of experiment before he got it just right. Like Alan McKirdy (*see* page 157), he recycles old piano keys when he can find them.

Barry enjoys looking round markets for materials he can recycle and finds the twice-weekly Loughborough market a useful source of supply of bits and pieces; there is often a box of old jewellery and he has occasionally found oddments of ivory. A visit to the antiques fair at Newark showground produced a broken Chinese dagger and an old teapot, both with ivory handles, and these provided enough raw material to miniaturize a 1920s ivory stool which he saw pictured in a Sotheby's catalogue, with some left over to use for inlay.

The variety and breadth of Barry's miniature work means

Above **Under construction: the pieces for a French *demi-lune* commode laid out ready for assembly.**

Below **Almost completed: the commode waiting for its hinges to be added. Barry saw the original commode at an antiques fair in Le Touquet, where he asked permission to photograph it.**

he uses many different materials beside the standard wood and metal. Marble and serpentine may be required as tops for commodes or tables. His local monumental masons cut marble for him into thin slices, but where serpentine is more appropriate, he is able to cut this softer material himself with a tile-saw blade which has tungsten carbide grit sintered (fused) to a steel wire. For ormolu decoration he carves brass with his engraving tools and then sends it off to be gold-plated.

Barry's restless imagination is always at work, thinking about what he might make next. Recently he discovered a book about Hawaiian furniture which is not, as I had supposed, primitive joinery made from driftwood. In fact it is sophisticated, inlaid furniture with many complex patterns, and tripod legs and fretwork which have something in common with New Orleans turn-of-the-century styles. 'Do you know anyone who is planning a Hawaiian-style dolls' house?' Barry asked me, with a gleam in his eye.

Charlotte Hunt
Swedish Style

During her childhood in Sweden, Charlotte Hunt thought of her sketching and painting as a hobby and never dreamed of becoming an artist. Even more unlikely was the prospect that she might become a specialist in painting delicate, neoclassical designs on miniature furniture, yet this is exactly what happened.

A family move meant that Charlotte finished her schooling in England, but there were many visits to a host of relations in country houses near Stockholm. Her earliest memories are of exquisite decorations in the Gustavian style, which is now her hallmark, and of the collections of tiny objects in her grandmother's home. She became fascinated by smallness, whether it was snuff boxes or silver and glass ornaments, and had plenty of opportunity to admire such things.

Painting remained a leisure interest until early in the 1980s when, one cold winter's day in Stockholm, Charlotte discovered a dolls' house shop. It was the first time she had seen such miniature furniture, or realized that it even existed. She became a firm friend of the owner of the shop and eventually brought an undecorated dolls' house back to England. It was in the Continental cabinet style, with a glass front, rather than an architectural facade, so that the small treasures inside would be visible. She decided to paint the interior in the style of a Swedish manor house, where paint is used to simulate marble, tapestry or even silk, while the panelled walls are painted with ribbon swags, flowers and fruit.

Swedish rooms had always been painted: peasant houses used bright, cheerful colours so that the interiors made a warm, glowing contrast to the icy wastes outside for much of the year. Furniture, too, even in aristocratic homes, was always painted rather than polished. Pine and birch were the only woods available to Swedish furniture makers,

so this was the only way to produce something really elegant.

In the eighteenth century the Swedish painters developed a more accomplished and sophisticated style, influenced by French work, but distinctly Nordic, which was much admired at the time and is still appreciated today. King Gustav III was largely responsible for establishing this new interest in the decorative arts, although, like his near contemporary, the Prince Regent of England, his artistic flair did not make him popular, and he was criticized for his

Above **Peasant-style painted decoration on a roomy cupboard. This style could be found in country manors and farmhouses from the end of the seventeenth century onwards.**

Left **A delicately painted chest of drawers with *faux* marble top, perhaps designed for a music room.**

extravagant tastes: his assassination was dramatized by Verdi in *The Masked Ball*.

In the 1980s 'Gustavian style' was taken up by interior decoration magazines in both England and America, which featured Swedish manor houses with their romantic neoclassical interiors. Charlotte became more and more interested, and read and learned as much as she could about the period. When a Swedish shop opened in Knightsbridge, London, selling reproduction eighteenth-century furniture, she began painting their full-size furniture, learning how to distress and glaze, to simulate marble in paint, and to add the typical flower designs.

When not busy with full-scale painting, Charlotte finished her dolls' house. Her enthusiasm was such that she went on to work for a dolls' house shop in London when they needed extra help, and she soon realized that there might be a niche for her talents in the miniature world, where she felt sure that Swedish-style painted furniture would be appreciated. She exhibited at the London Dollshouse Festival in 1985, not showing her own work, which at that time was intended only for her own dolls' house, but representing the shop in Stockholm, displaying Swedish stoves and

A marble-top console table with elaborate gilded swags.

painted furniture in a room setting she had designed and decorated for the show.

Soon after that, the dolls' house shop in Stockholm closed when its owner retired, but for Charlotte that first fair had already been the real beginning of her new career. She found someone to teach her how to make furniture, and has always learned how to make every new piece in her range herself, although she does not regard its actual construction as central to her craft. Instead, she now has the furniture made to her design, while she concentrates on the painting and upholstery.

After her training in full-size techniques, she found she needed to make some alterations in the way she worked in order to suit 1/12 scale. She still uses a mix of oil-based paints to make a good foundation for the decorative designs, and says she has to be careful about ventilation in her workroom as the fumes become very strong when working for a long period. The first coat is left to dry out thoroughly for a day before she distresses it to get an antique look, and then she uses water-based paints and fine sable brushes to add the swags, flowers and ribbon decoration. Charlotte takes immense trouble and time to achieve her effects, which, like the originals, appear almost three-dimensional. Finally, each piece is protected with a glaze of waterproof paint.

For the upholstered furniture in both the Louis XV and Louis XVI styles, which were so wholeheartedly adopted by the Swedes, she uses pure silk fabrics from France, and exceptionally fine cotton in minute checks or stripes. If she cannot find exactly what she needs, she hand-paints the design on to fine material. Looking at one of her flower-strewn patterns, I realized that this would sometimes be necessary – the tiny delicate flowers seemed to be distributed in a random yet controlled fashion, which could never be achieved by the repetitive process employed in printing. Her braid and trimmings are specially made to tone with the fabrics.

Charlotte wanted to cover the whole field of eighteenth-century Swedish interiors in miniature, and no Swedish home of the period would be complete without its focal point, the huge stove which made a house habitable in the freezing winters. The finest stoves were made at the Marieberg factory in Stockholm, and were renowned for both their efficiency and the beauty of their ceramic tiles of pure white, decorated in blue or with pastel-coloured flowers. The stoves were not made in any great quantity, and there are only 30 still in existence, of which no fewer than 17 are at Sturehov, near Stockholm, a manor house that Charlotte particularly likes. She has miniaturized the most striking stove still remaining at Sturehov, as well as smaller

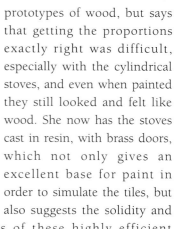

Above **Regency exoticism – X-frame stool with leopard seat.**

Below **A typical white-painted chair with blue-and-white striped covering.**

models. At first she made her prototypes of wood, but says that getting the proportions exactly right was difficult, especially with the cylindrical stoves, and even when painted they still looked and felt like wood. She now has the stoves cast in resin, with brass doors, which not only gives an excellent base for paint in order to simulate the tiles, but also suggests the solidity and massiveness of these highly efficient heating devices.

Charlotte's favourite display unit is a room setting made for her by Mulvany & Rogers (*see page 21*), copied from the Parrot Room in Sturehov. Like many of the rooms there, the original decorations were by Lars Bolander, perhaps the most famous decorative artist during the reign of King Gustav III. The room gets its name from the parrot that Bolander painted among the foliage and flowers on one of the wall panels, and Charlotte has reproduced this in her miniature. In general she does not copy exactly, but tries to interpret a design in her own way so that each wall painting is unique. One of her room settings was done specially for the Doll and Toy Museum in Rothenberg, Germany.

Charlotte still feels a nostalgic longing for Sweden, although her home is now in London. It is the special quality of the light that she misses: 'When you come into a Swedish manor house, the first impression is of light and

brightness.' Such houses are almost always built by water, with a lake reflecting more light through the long windows and, for so much of the year, from the snow outside. Because of the dark winters it was important to retain as much light in the rooms as possible, to be picked up by the soft colours of the painted walls, furniture and even ceilings. Bleached pine floorboards without any covering also helped to lighten the interiors – although they can seem very cold.

When the weather in England is dull and wet, Charlotte goes to visit friends in Spain, taking her work with her. There she finds another version of the light she craves. But in summer she enjoys her English garden. She is a passionate gardener and now finds inspiration for her paintings in her English flowers, especially the old-fashioned roses which are her favourites.

Opposite **The Parrot Room from Sturehov, made by Mulvany & Rogers with painted panels by Charlotte. The room is elegantly furnished with Charlotte's 'Antoinette' seating.**

Above **A selection of Charlotte's stoves. The rectangular stove on the left is the finest Marieberg stove remaining at Sturehov. The wooden feet on these early stoves were later banned because of the risk of fire.**

John and Jean Morgan
Shaker Simplicity

It may seem surprising to find a former industrial chemist making miniature Shaker furniture, but not entirely inappropriate. Many of those who went from England to America to form the first Shaker community, in 1774, left behind very different occupations.

The Shaker sect has now all but died out, but its furniture designs have survived and are becoming ever more popular. Shaker furniture is simple, beautifully made and practical. It was made for use, not ornament, and fits in with almost any decorative style; this applies in miniature as well as full size.

John Morgan says he began making Shaker furniture by accident, not design. After working in the plastics industry he switched to marketing, and became marketing director for the UK branch of a large chemical company specializing in

plastics for wrapping foodstuffs. In 1981 he went to the Netherlands to set up the company's operation there, and soon found he was not only marketing director but also project manager. Enough was enough, and after doing two jobs at once for a while he decided he wanted a change. The opportunity came when his company merged with another, and he was able to leave on his own terms.

It was while he was working in the Netherlands that John took to making wooden models. 'I had to keep sane somehow,' he says. His first miniatures were of boats, as sea canoeing is his main leisure interest, shared with his wife, Jean, who introduced him to the sport. He had already made several of their full-size canoes, and a smaller one for the children.

He then tried out some model furniture kits and spent time working out how to achieve a perfect finish, experimenting with a variety of finishing techniques. On his mantelpiece he still has a miniature cradle and a tiny chest of drawers that pre-date his interest in Shaker. That began after his return to England, when, at the Practical Woodworking Exhibition at Wembley, he bought a copy of *Modelling and Miniature Crafts* magazine, and came across an article on how to make a Shaker rocking chair. In the same issue of the magazine there was an advertisement for the newly opened Shaker Shop in London, which sells imported Shaker-style furniture and accessories. A visit to the shop was inspiring, he said, and he

went on to read all he could about Shaker furniture, with the idea of making miniature replicas for his own amusement.

Soon after that he went to the London Dollshouse Festival for the first time, and discovered there was no Shaker-style furniture among the miniatures on show there, nor at other shows he went to. He realized that if no one was making Shaker furniture, perhaps he could find his own niche in the miniature world. But he felt that he would need to improve his skills. In 1990 he decided to go to a summer school on making miniature furniture, held at Bradford

University. This was helpful in that he was able to try out more power tools than he had in his own workshop at home, but, most important, he learned that he was way beyond the beginner's stage. While still in Bradford he met the organizer of the Leeds Dolls' House and Miniature Fair and was encouraged to exhibit some of his Shaker pieces. To his delight, they proved very popular.

John now exhibits at many major miniatures fairs, where some of his best customers are American. His furniture is also on sale in the museum shop of the American Museum in Bath, where there is a fine collection of full-size Shaker furniture. In 1992 the museum collection was supplemented by additional pieces on loan from the Metropolitan Museum in New York for a special exhibition; John contacted the curator, who was immediately interested in the idea of stocking the miniatures in the museum shop to coincide with the exhibition, and John was able to visit the museum and study original pieces he had not seen before.

Perhaps the best known piece of Shaker furniture today is the chair. Thomas Merton said, 'The peculiar grace of a Shaker chair is due to the maker's belief that an angel might come and sit on it.' Although this is a lovely idea, the chairs have a strong basic

Right **A room setting with good use made of the peg rail to hang small items of furniture: a chair and cupboard.**

Opposite **Two rocking chairs in a Shaker room setting.**

construction, while the stretchers are very slender to lessen the weight. When not in use they were, like many other pieces, hung on peg rail fixed around the room, and the light construction made it easier to move them around.

The chairs are where Jean Morgan makes her essential contribution to the Simply Shaker enterprise. She has always had her own career as a teacher – in the Netherlands she learned to speak Dutch as soon as possible and then taught English to adult students. Now she specializes in another sort of teaching, working in the occupational therapy department of the Royal National Orthopaedic Hospital spinal injuries unit.

But she, too, soon became fascinated by Shaker furniture and somehow she finds time to weave the seats and backs for the chairs and stools which John makes.

The Shakers used tape, which they found easier to work than rush or cane, and more durable. The tape was dyed, using only natural plant dyes, and woven into herringbone and chequerboard patterns. Blue and red were the easiest colours to produce, but in muted tones, which elsewhere in the nineteenth century were supplanted by the brighter aniline dyes. Now the more subtle shades are back in favour. Like the Shakers, Jean dyes her own 'tape' to achieve the authentic colours, using slightly

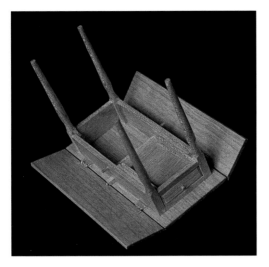

Left The neatness of John's jointing can be seen in this table.

Right The Shaker house designed by John Morgan and Jeremy Collins, available from Gable End Designs.

Below The interior of the Shaker house.

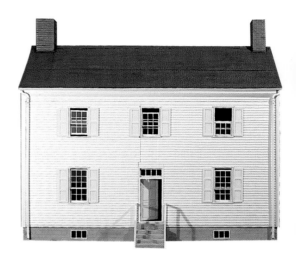

textured ½in (2mm) wide rayon ribbon.

The seats have two layers of weaving and the original chairs were sometimes provided with a horsehair cushion in between the two layers, to pad the seat. In 1/12 scale, where there is no room for a cushion, achieving the

double layer of weaving neatly and also getting the tension just right was at first difficult to achieve. In addition, the chair seats taper towards the back so that at the rear corners the tape has to overlap invisibly, to ensure that the chequerboard pattern looks correct. With patient practice, Jean eventually found that she had mastered the technique and now finds it straightforward, if time-consuming. Each chair seat takes over 6ft (2m) of ribbon to complete.

Shaker furniture was made in maple or cherry. John finds cherry wood the best for miniature pieces as it is very close-grained. He buys thick planks at least a year before he uses them, storing them in carefully controlled conditions to allow the moisture content to reach the same humidity as the average room. Eventually the wood is cut into smaller sections ready for use.

To reproduce the slim lines of Shaker furniture in 1/12 scale means using precision machinery. A door in John and Jean's neat sitting room opens into an equally neat and tidy workshop. There he has a band saw, a small circular saw, an engineer's lathe, a drilling machine and a milling machine, a router with very fine cutters and a large 4ft (1.2m) planer–thicknesser. In addition, he has a jeweller's saw, which he finds ideal for giving a perfect, clean cut. He has modified his router, mounting it upside down into the worktable so that he can cut the grooves for rebates easily and with complete accuracy, and makes his own chisels by grinding and sharpening masonry nails, in order to cut a ½5in (1mm) wide mortise.

John's workshop is surprisingly dust-free. 'I'm allergic to dust,' he told me. He makes inventive use of old vacuum cleaners, fixing them as dust collectors to extract all the dust from the bottom of both his bandsaw and circular saw with a neatly made attachment.

Perfect jointing is essential and John takes a pride in the fact that his furniture looks equally good from every angle, even upside down. Because all the joints are on view, he says, it is in some ways more akin to model engineering than to conventional woodworking. He uses engineer's calipers to measure to ⅟₁₀₀₀in (0.025mm). This degree of

accuracy means that if you take a drawer from one piece and put it into another, it will still fit. Drawers are rebated, not dovetailed: because Shaker furniture contains so many drawers and John's range of pieces continues to increase, it would not be practicable to make dovetails and still keep pace with orders. John makes his own room boxes and display units, ready fitted with peg rail to provide an instant Shaker room setting for those who have not yet graduated to an entire Shaker house, but want to display their collection in the traditional manner. However, he felt that it would be nice if

people could have an entire house at a modest cost to furnish appropriately.

In 1993 John suggested to Jeremy Collins, who specializes in miniature buildings assembled from moulded parts, that they might collaborate on designing just such a house, and the end result of their discussions and planning is now available in kit form (as well as fully finished) from Jeremy at Gable End Designs (*see* page 181). John supplies all the peg rail to be built into the model which Jeremy has perfected and produced, and no doubt a great deal of John's furniture will be destined for the finished houses.

The most instantly recognizable Shaker accessory is the oval box, skilfully made and fixed with copper nails in a similar way to the English trug. These boxes were used for storing pulses, dried herbs and seeds.

Patrick Puttock
English Country Furniture

Patrick Puttock was a regular army officer when he first began making models of English warships. His home was in Devon, a county with many centuries of naval tradition, so perhaps it is not surprising that his long-standing enjoyment led him to move on to extremely fine and accurate models of ships – in his case, those which served during the Napoleonic wars.

His first ship model, the *Brigantine Leon* (of a slightly later period than his eventual specialization), was sold at Christie's to a foreign newspaper tycoon, who afterwards bought every model ship that Patrick made. Each time he returned to Devon with a completed model, his buyer would send his private plane to collect it. However, although collection was easy for the customer, Patrick found it quite difficult transporting his large models back from Hong Kong, or wherever he might be, and he began to think he should make something smaller.

When he was in England, Patrick also enjoyed collecting English country furniture. He always liked best the sort of antiques that you find in people's homes, not those of museum quality, but good, honest pieces with the patina of use, and perhaps even slightly battered. He decided that some of his favourite pieces from his own home would be ideal for miniaturization. His years of naval model-making meant that he knew how to draw plans, and to work with both wood and metal to very exact specifications in small scale. So after a certain amount of experimentation he made a bow-fronted chest of drawers which satisfied his high standards. Luckily he had chosen 1/12 scale, although he cannot now remember why: he never took advice on it, and it seems to have been pure chance.

At that time Patrick was still serving as ground liaison officer attached to an RAF squadron in Germany, but when he came home on leave, someone mentioned that there was to be a local dolls' house, crafts

Opposite **Patrick in his workshop, with two partly completed bureaux.**

Left
A Hepplewhite toilet mirror, *circa* 1780, on a late-eighteenth-century bow-fronted chest of drawers in mahogany.

and miniatures fair in the West Country. By then he had completed a number of pieces of miniature furniture, all made with his characteristic care and precision, and he decided to take a stand at the fair and see what the public thought of his work. It was admired, he says, but he didn't sell any. Other stallholders told him he should be exhibiting such high quality work at a larger,

more specialized fair. After this he made further enquiries, and as a result was offered a table at the London Dollshouse Festival, where he did extremely well and took enough orders to keep him busy for some time.

Patrick was encouraged and pleased by the success of his first venture into the dolls' house field, and began to think seriously

about making miniature furniture full time when he left the Army. He exhibited at other major fairs and when orders continued to come in, from America as well as Britain, he felt the decision had been made for him and he relinquished his commission. By this time he had perfected a range of pieces which he can repeat to order, some still based on his own full-size eighteenth- and nineteenth-century furniture, and others copied from furniture he had seen in Devon and Somerset antiques shops.

He is attracted to eighteenth- and early-nineteenth-century mahogany- and walnut-veneered pieces. The hand-cut veneers of that period were much thicker than those used today, and he likes to reproduce this handmade effect, making the very best use of the grain in the same way as the earlier craftsman. His American customers will often order something that had been made in mahogany, but specify burr walnut, which is much prized in America for its interesting colour and grain, so for these commissions Patrick has to search out the most beautifully figured burr he can find. Mahogany veneer is actually more difficult to work than walnut, as it has a tendency to split, particularly when making up a serpentine shape, but he finds that it is the stringing and crossbanding that take the most time and patience because of the minute scale.

Although most of his furniture is copied directly from the original antique, I was surprised to learn that a piecrust-edged pedestal table which I admired was actually based on a modern reproduction. This type of tilt-top table became popular in the mid-eighteenth century and would have been made in mahogany. Patrick's miniature was made in boxwood, which is so dense that it is sometimes difficult to tell which way the grain is running before cutting. Using this wood eliminates the possibility of an unsuitable grain size, and means that the miniature will be exceptionally smooth and tactile.

Patrick first made a template and then carved out the elaborate piecrust edge by hand, with a chisel, in the same way that an eighteenth-century table would have been made. A machine-made reproduction generally lacks the depth of carving which is achieved by handwork – this was certainly true of the one on which he based his design – so the result was that his model was infinitely superior.

Queen Anne tallboy – a chest on a stand – in one piece because it is more convenient for people to handle, although the original had a separate stand so that the height could be reduced if the piece needed to be moved.

Looking at the perfectly matching set of mahogany chairs, I wondered whether Patrick found it tedious making a complete set. 'On the contrary,' he says, 'it's very satisfying.' He likes making chairs, particularly sturdy country chairs like the

Opposite
A Victorian mahogany bureau bookcase with glazed, barred doors. This piece dates from around 1870 and is decorated throughout with ebony and boxwood stringing.

Left
A Chippendale-style piecrust-edged tilt-top table on a pedestal stand, with a small oak table, *circa* 1700, with drawer and turned legs.

He also miniaturizes pieces from other people's homes – an elegant mahogany dining table and set of chairs is copied from those belonging to his mother-in-law. The original table has an extending leaf which can be fitted in when additional guests are expected, and although Patrick included this feature at first, later versions of the table are made in one piece. This is because the limited space of a dolls' house does not usually allow room to seat extra guests, and one customer told him that she had trouble dusting it without dislodging the loose section. For the same reason, he makes a

oak chair in his own sitting room, with its claw-like ends to the arm rests and a strong, upright back. 'It's not all that comfortable,' he mentioned, and when I sat on it I was able to confirm that – but I could imagine a farmer sitting impressively upright on the hard chair to pay out the week's wages to his farmhands.

Patrick is happiest working to commission when he is asked to miniaturize something from the customer's own home. He says it is more difficult to get the proportions right if he hasn't actually seen the piece, as he likes to measure each dimension. However he will work from a photograph or drawing if necessary. He made an attractive French provincial-style chair after being sent a photocopy of a drawing from a book as his only reference material.

Patrick's daughter, Caroline, has taken over the upholstery and fitting of the covers to the Queen Anne dining chairs. Caroline is

and Patrick says, with typical British understatement, that there was quite a lot of clearing up to do when he moved in. Now it contains a Unimat lathe and a Hegner saw, which Patrick finds invaluable to cut the templates he needs in order to reproduce chair legs for sets of Queen Anne chairs. The workshop is also used for the metalwork he still enjoys, although at present this is

Good country furniture: a solid oak chair, *circa* 1850, with carved arms and pierced back splat. The corner chair dates from around 1700 and has cabriole legs and ball-and-claw feet.

studying graphic design at university so her upholstery work is limited to the vacations. At first, she said, she found it very difficult, but she persevered. The main problem is that she uses very fine silk, and if it frays even slightly the cover has to be scrapped and she has to start again with a fresh piece. She prefers to use old silk and keeps a look-out for anything suitable in antique markets.

Patrick's home, the Old Crown Inn, is a former Somerset cider house and his workshop used to be the former skittle alley. The previous owner used it to keep goats in,

mainly limited to making handles and hinges – replicas of the more unusual ones fitted to some original country furniture. Many makers of miniature furniture buy in such items from specialist makers (*see* page 122), as designs taken from town furniture used more standardized fittings. Patrick's experience in metalwork, for his model ships and steam engines, meant that he already knew how to approach this. Even so, he read as much as he could about the way in which metal fittings were made in the eighteenth and nineteenth centuries, and then did some experimenting to perfect his techniques. He cuts out the back plate from sheet brass, turns two fixing pins individually, and adds engraving if needed. Oval handles are more difficult to fit than round ones, as there are two pins. If the holes for fixing the handle on to the back plate are out of true by as little as the thickness of a hair, the handle will look slightly crooked, whereas there is no trouble with ring handles that have only a single pin.

Years of reading and prowling round antiques shops mean that Patrick has a connoisseur's appreciation of English country furniture; he talks about the pieces he admires with knowledge and enthusiasm. His commitment to reproducing the feeling

Left **Contrasting styles in French chairs – Louis XVI and a Provincial-style carved and painted country chair.**

Below **Patrick's daughter, Caroline, holding a three-seater sofa which she has just upholstered.**

of the original means that he spends many hours cleaning up, polishing and then dulling each piece to achieve just the right degree of patina and feeling of use. Making a model of a modern piece of furniture with a matt finish would not interest him at all. For someone who loves old furniture, there is an intangible delight in seeing a fine piece which has been looked after in a family home for several generations, still standing in the same position in a room, and handling one of Patrick's models gives a similar feeling of pleasure.

Colin & Yvonne
Roberson
Furnishings in Metal

Bamboo furniture has had successive waves of popularity ever since the Prince Regent used it to furnish his exotic Royal Pavilion in Brighton. In the Victorian era, no parlour was fully furnished without its clutter of occasional tables, and during the 1920s and '30s bamboo moved into the garden, with variations on Chinese Chippendale chairs and tables. Such furniture might be difficult to obtain in 1/12 scale, as bamboo is not grown in miniature size.

Luckily for those dolls' house owners who want a touch of chinoiserie in their stylish rooms, one of the specialities of Colin and Yvonne Roberson is *faux* bamboo, made in metal, which looks like the real thing but is more hard-wearing. Colin points out that he is, in fact, following historical precedent with his use of metal. Even in the Royal Pavilion at Brighton, all is not what it seems: one of the most striking features is the

elegant 'bamboo' staircase which turns out, on closer inspection, to be cast iron.

Colin made his first miniature brass bed in 1978, and it was to prove a turning point in what he can claim to have been a flourishing career as a struggling artist – although he admits that he never actually did have to starve in a garret! After his foundation year at art school, he had to give up his studies to help his father in the family business. Eventually, a job welding model aircraft introduced him to metalwork, which led, in turn, to a change of direction from painting to metal sculpture.

He sold his work through a local craft gallery, and his first miniature brass bed was made to oblige someone who had bought one of his full-size sculpted figures. When the customer told him about the dolls' house hobby, Colin began to wonder whether he could use his skills in metalwork to produce something saleable. After trying several different styles in period beds, he next made some brass and copper containers with metal replicas of foliage plants, and then a selection of grates, fireplaces, stoves and geysers.

One difficulty in expanding the range was to think of ways of simulating other materials in metal, but Colin was always good at lateral thinking and realized that 'bamboo' furniture might work well. This proved to be the case. At this stage, busy with three young children, Yvonne's only contribution had been to paint the plant leaves green, but she encouraged Colin to pursue the idea. When he sold some of those early designs to a dolls' house shop and received a repeat order, it began to seem a practical proposition. By the

time their children were at school, Yvonne was as much involved as Colin, and gradually took over the painting and finishing of all the miniatures.

Ever since playing with his own collection of Dinky toys as a child, Colin has had a weakness for miniature wheeled vehicles, so his range soon expanded to include a variety of period bicycles – a Harrod's delivery bicycle is perhaps the most popular, and Yvonne says she has long since lost count of the number of times she has painted 'Harrods' on a bicycle nameplate.

The chance discovery, while on holiday, of a comprehensive private collection of

period perambulators and baby carriages gave them the idea of reproducing some of these attractive designs for the accommodation of the 1/12 scale baby; it was especially helpful that the owner had also written an illustrated book.

After making working drawings for each new design, Colin starts by making the templates and jigs for the separate parts of each model. He uses 24-gauge mild steel,

the Victorian bedsteads are made from brass rods in a variety of thicknesses, and Colin prefers to do this by eye and then shape each of them by hand.

To make wheels, he uses copper-coated mild steel welding rods which he buys in 15lb (7 kg) packs, each rod about 30in (75cm) long. To turn this into a wheel, he first bends the metal rod round the jig to make a circle, and snips it off. Each spoke

An elegant period perambulator, with lace-trimmed hood and quilted lining.

which he buys in sheets of about 6ft x 3ft (2m x 1m). The sections of furniture and the perambulator bodies are all cut by hand, using a template and jeweller's tin-snips. Any thicker gauge of metal would be impossible to cut using this method; even this requires a strong grip. The elaborate scrolled tops for

has to be cut accurately and is then fitted into the tiny jig and silver-soldered in place. The repetitive task of making four wheels for each pram, with 12 spokes to each wheel, could all too easily become tedious. But, he says, all this endless spoking of wheels does give him the time he needs to think up new ideas. He tries to introduce one new item at each dolls' house fair he attends.

The whole process, from shaped metal to finished product, is long, and it is during the later stages that Yvonne takes over. First she removes all remaining traces of the soft, waxy flux left from the metalwork. A few minutes in boiling water will remove most of it, but to get it out of all the corners she needs to give it a good scrub with a toothbrush in hot, soapy water. The cleaned metal is left to dry overnight and is then ready to paint. First she applies an undercoat of red oxide, then the main colour and finally gold decoration for the 'bamboo' pieces, or tiny flower designs for *papier-mâché*, one of their more recent ideas. For some of the beds where there is a large centre panel to be decorated, Colin may join in again to take his share of the painting.

There are four stages in painting a perambulator: first the main body, but leaving it with undercoat only at the places where the leather will later be fitted, and next the undercarriage and wheels. The handle is painted last. The bifurcated rivets to attach the hood also have to be painted before that can be fitted. They now make about a dozen different models of period perambulator and Yvonne also does the leatherwork.

Like Colin, she uses templates, to cut her chair seats, pram interiors and hoods, all from the best quality washable glove leather. The next stage is for the pieces to be buttoned by stitching through on to a backing, before being glued in place. The

hoods are shaped on a wooden block before being attached to a metal frame, and finished with lace trimming. Yvonne also makes the neatly buttoned mattresses for the beds and simulates cane chair seats from double-thread canvas, which is thinner than real cane. She has never had any formal training in craft work and has achieved her current standard of excellence by patience and perseverance. One skill she hasn't yet

mastered is miniature cane work, and the baskets for the bicycles are supplied by specialist Shirley Edwards.

Gardens are another source of inspiration: Colin's workshop in their own garden began life as a modest-sized garden shed. He was delighted to see the new interest in dolls' house gardens and during one winter, when most gardeners would have been reading their seed catalogues, he began designing garden furniture – as usual, in many different styles, ranging from green-painted folding tables, chairs and benches based on those seen in his local park, to the

A chair in simulated bamboo, cream painted and based on those that are in the Queen's sitting room in Queen Mary's dolls' house. The plant in the plantstand is also made in metal, and the garden seat is upholstered in painted silk.

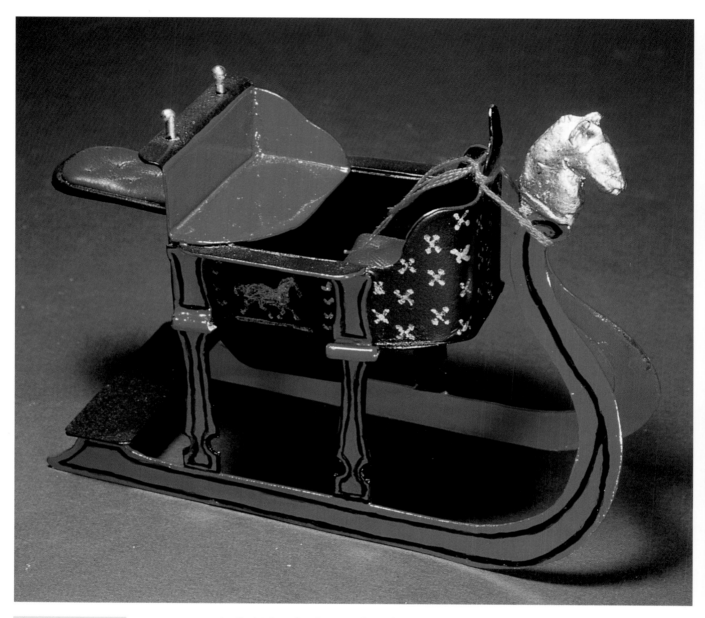

The Russian child's sleigh.

more exotic Gothick-style chairs and garden seats that would complement an eighteenth-century doll's house. When he saw the wonderful period lawnmowers in the garden of Queen Mary's dolls' house, he decided to make a lawnmower of his own: not quite such a grand model as some of those regal mowers, he says, but the sort of hand-propelled mower that was used by most people from the 1920s through to the '40s, with a box to hold the clippings. It is not a fully working model – and although there

are blades which rotate, they will not actually trim the pile of your carpet. Colin's machines are artistic interpretations of the real thing, not precision-made replicas.

There is no shortage of ideas in the Roberson household, but they are always willing to consider ideas from other people by way of special commissions. When I showed Colin an advertisement for a Russian child's sleigh, dated 1840, which was to be sold at auction by Spink's, he looked at the illustration a little doubtfully at first. I persuaded him to take away the picture, which showed an exotically painted gold-and-black sleigh with scarlet runners and a gilded horse's head with reins attached for the child to hold. Sure enough, the following day he sat down and worked out the design, and at the next miniatures fair they attended, they brought it with them and displayed it on their stand ready for me to collect. But before I did so, they had already taken a substantial order from an American customer for more (*see* page 83).

A commission from their local dolls' house shop which produced further orders was for the interior of a traditional fish-and-chip shop, complete with fryers, counter and even the shop owner. By this stage, Colin had already been thinking about making a few dolls, as he wanted something novel to show on the stand at miniatures fairs which would make a contrast to the metal miniatures, and might also amuse the customers. He went on to model some character dolls which show his keen sense of humour. Sculptors work in many media, but modelling in Fimo is probably one of the lesser-known art forms, he says. However it does offer him yet another diversion from making wheels and the dolls he forms

The fish-and-chip shop counter. Humour always lurks just below the surface in the Roberson workshop.

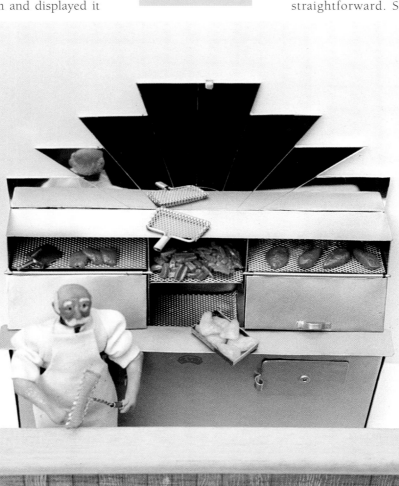

with it are certainly popular.

Colin and Yvonne sell their work through shops on the Continent as well as in Britain, the United States and Australia. Yvonne deals with all the paperwork. At first it seemed complicated but she soon discovered it was really quite straightforward. She has a useful tip for other miniaturists going into the export market. 'Never use a main post office, they simply don't have the time to be interested.' She has sorted out all her difficulties in mailing by always going to the same, small, local post office, where they are not too busy to be helpful by supplying the correct forms. She adds that it is very important never to get behind with the paperwork or there will be problems with the yearly accounts and tax returns.

She has always been careful about packing, but is now extra fussy, since the occasion when they sent a single brass bed to a customer and it arrived with a bent leg. Fortunately, that customer, too, had a sense of humour and was not put out: she wrote to say that the bed was perfect for her dolls' house scullery maid, who hated getting up in the morning – so much so that she always gave one of the bed legs a good kick!

Ivan Turner
The Elizabethan Specialist

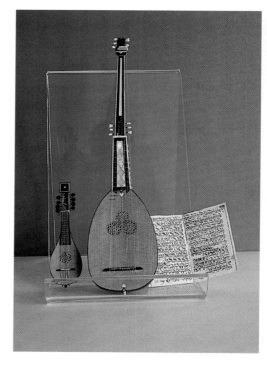

Ivan Turner is unique among the miniaturists featured in this book in that he does not sell his work – it will all eventually go to a museum to form a collection of 1/12 scale miniature furniture covering the period 1200–1690.

He had always been fascinated by the Elizabethan period, but his interest in medieval and Tudor furniture really developed from his earlier delight in music-making: in the 1970s this led him to abandon the piano in favour of the lute. The instruments used by the members of the Lute Society are all, of necessity, reproductions. Ivan wanted to know how they were made and, as a member, had access to the scale drawings made by modern lutemakers. This interest would later resurface in his miniature work, but for many years it was just an enjoyable hobby. He was far too busy with his job as personnel director of a large packing and stationery group in Bristol to put it to any practical use.

As part of his work, Ivan always advised the firm's employees to plan their retirements carefully, but when he himself took early retirement, it was a snap decision. At first, his new leisure seemed quite enough and it was pure chance, in the form of a short television item, that pointed him towards the work which would eventually take over his retirement. In the programme, leading British miniaturist Denis Hillman (*see* caption, page 1) discussed his own speciality: furniture in the styles of Louis XV and XVI. Impressed by the skill and dedication that went into making each tiny piece, Ivan decided to try something himself. When he heard that Denis was giving a seminar on inlay, he went along and took his first – very amateur, he says – piece with him, made to a scale of 1/10. His talent must have shown itself in that first attempt, and Denis encouraged him to try the more accepted 1/12 scale.

Ivan's interest in Elizabethan music and the history of the period had by now extended to the furniture, and in particular inlaid work,

but he soon discovered that there is a shortage of written information about the working methods of the furniture makers of the time. Eventually he came across a book by Victor Chinnery, consultant on oak furniture at Sotheby's, and this gave him the most authoritative and detailed information that he could find, enabling him to make his miniatures as authentic as possible.

The early Tudors were learning to make decorative domestic furniture for the first time: instead of devoting their artistic talents solely to ecclesiastical and court work, they were developing new skills and techniques. Some of this early domestic furniture can still be found and studied in museums. Much of it was roughly made. It was standard practice, for example, for the floor and sides of a chest to be simply butted together and

The Nonsuch chest, Ivan's first 1/12 scale miniature.

The magnificent Corbet bed. The counterpane was embroidered by Daphne Turner on linen-backed silk. She based her design on one at Hardwick Hall, and used 32ft (9.7m) of gold and silver thread couched double. Like her husband's work, Daphne's too is of museum quality.

nailed. Where nailed joints are called for, Ivan uses fine entomological pins, first filing down the heads.

From about 1500 the knowledge of how to make dovetails and mortise-and-tenon joints gradually spread until they became standard practice and these better-made pieces became known as 'joined' chests. At this time the English joiners still lagged behind their continental counterparts, whose work at this time was more sophisticated, although this was soon to change.

Every schoolchild knows about Henry VIII's personal life; but the King was also a cultivated patron who promoted the interchange of artistic ideas with the Continent. During his reign, Italian, Dutch and Flemish artists and craftsmen were encouraged to come to England. As a result, the English joiners learned continental techniques and began to make elaborate, decorative furniture that was more richly carved and inlaid. Furniture that until then had been purely utilitarian, such as the large, heavy chests that could be locked to secure valuables, was now given the new 'markatree'

front that soon became a test of the craftsman's skill.

Ivan had seen a Nonsuch chest in a local museum, the Red Lodge, in Bristol, and felt that to attempt one of these remarkable pieces would be a challenge – in fact, for a beginner it might seem an impossibility. However he studied other examples in the Victoria & Albert Museum and the Museum of London and decided to go ahead. He feels there is no substitute for looking at the original piece before attempting to reproduce it in miniature scale. He did his research

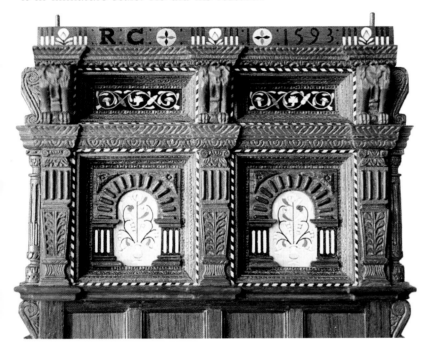

thoroughly and found the museum curators helpful when he explained what he wanted to do. He emphasizes the need to make an appointment, explain in advance in writing why you want to study a piece in detail, and if possible, take something you have already made with you.

He had set himself an additional problem in tackling such a complicated piece: he would also need to make a replica of an authentic sixteenth-century lock. As a starting point, Denis Hillman showed him

Guilloche, resembling a twisted, two-colour rope, outlines the panels on the headboard – it is one of the most effective of this type of running design.

how he made miniature versions of eighteenth-century locks. Ivan then contacted Chubb, the old-established locksmiths, to obtain further information from their archivist, and supplemented that with visits to the Science Museum in London and the Willenhall Lock Museum. After much practice he perfected the making of locks for sixteenth- and seventeenth-century miniature furniture, but with one essential anachronism: the original locks would have been made in wrought iron, but in 1/12 scale this would be too easily bent out of shape, so instead he uses mild steel which he blackens with 'metal black'.

Ivan decided right from the start what he was aiming for: a reproduction, as exact as he could make it, of the piece as it would have looked when new. He uses no ageing techniques. It is astonishing to look at one of Ivan's miniatures, with all its diversity of beautifully coloured woods inlaid in complicated, geometrical and floral patterns, and realize that the blackened oak of sixteenth-century furniture, as we see it today, must once have looked equally light and cheerful. His decision to copy pieces as they would have looked when newly made means that he uses many of the same natural woods as those in the original inlay: ebony, box, sycamore, walnut, holly and apple. The only wood he colours is sycamore, which he stains green where necessary – for leaves in a floral design, for example.

His representation of a spectacular bed is copied from one made for the Corbet family in 1593. It was designed for their house in Meriden, Warwickshire, and later moved to the family home near Shrewsbury, when Sir Richard Corbet became High Sheriff of Shropshire. Ivan was able to study the bed in Rowley's House Museum in Shrewsbury, where it is currently on loan from the Victoria & Albert Museum. Like many of the finest pieces of Elizabethan furniture, it is made in walnut. Walnut is much more liable to attack by woodworm than oak, so it is remarkable that this ancient bed has survived.

Ivan was lucky when a miniaturist friend gave him some 100-year-old walnut that was exactly the colour and tone he needed. Walnut can be carved much more crisply than oak, in which the large pores make it difficult to reproduce accurate detail in the miniature scale, so it was essential to use the correct wood for this intricately carved piece. There are three rows of geometric carving on each of the two mouldings round the top of the tester and four on each deep moulding surrounding the panels on the bedhead. He grinds away part of a needle intended for sewing canvas to use as a carving tool for this type of work.

After studying the original bed carefully Ivan was able to work out what other woods had been used besides walnut. The decorative panels on the headboard are now almost as dark as the rest but he found a tiny piece had broken off at the edge of a panel and discovered that it was, in fact, sycamore. The sycamore is inlaid with vases of holly and box, flowers of holly and yew and stems of bog oak. The shading of the vases and petals was done by singeing the pieces with a small electric soldering iron, to simulate scorching by hot sand.

Perfection has its limitations: on rare occasions Ivan may decide to leave out a line of inlay that in 1/12 scale would be so fine that it would be almost invisible to the naked eye; for this reason he left out one miniscule

The Cologne cupboard: a fine example of continental workmanship.

line of sycamore next to the four mouldings surrounding the panels. The two dark, horizontal panels are made of bog oak; if you look carefully, Ivan told me, you will see that they are not identical. The original craftsman missed out one leaf on the right-hand panel, so Ivan intentionally omitted this one, too.

Seeing Ivan's miniature of this splendid bed with its light-coloured panels gives an indication that Elizabethan interiors were not all the dark, gloomy places so many of them now appear. One Elizabethan house which is flooded with light and where the rooms are spacious and colourful is Hardwick Hall in Derbyshire, built in the final years of the sixteenth century. The impression given by this amazing house with it huge windows is of the ideals of an ultra-modern architect translated into the Elizabethan vernacular.

Southwark and Norwich were two centres of furniture-making in Tudor England, but it was in an antiques shop in Gloucestershire that Ivan discovered the very fine cupboard (now in a private collection) that he believes was made by one of the immigrant craftsmen from Cologne. The quality and precision of the inlay are typical of the best continental work. The native English craftsmen, at least in the early part of that period, were not so meticulous. Repetitive patterns of inlay, such as geometric strips, were made up by specialist makers and could be bought 'off the shelf' in the same way as today we may buy mouldings from a DIY store. On English-made pieces the marquetry patterns were often fitted in to length but without making a careful join at the corners and squares were sometimes cut to fit the available space. Ivan copies these imperfections in his miniature pieces. He makes all his own mouldings by hand, using a home-made miniature scratch-stock, so that they have a handmade rather than a machine-made appearance.

Although at first Ivan concentrated on English and German furniture, he was interested by the way in which Renaissance design influenced the English work and eventually he decided to make an Italian marriage chest, or *cassone*. These were usually made in pairs, heavily gilded and as rich-looking as the craftsman could make them. In the early sixteenth century a leading artist would be commissioned to paint the front and side panels to be set into these chests, but by about 1650 the paintings were, instead, reproduced in marquetry.

Ivan's *cassone* is one of the few pieces which he has not copied directly from a still-existing piece of furniture, although it is typical of those of the period. His inlaid design is based on a painting that was clearly done for a *cassone* by Piero della Francesca, which is in the Museum Nationale in Urbino, and shows an idealized townscape. The three-dimensional effect must have seemed astonishing at that time, when the Renaissance artists had newly rediscovered perspective. Ivan made full-size drawings for this design so that he could take measurements accurately and then scale down the dimensions. His work is so perfectly done that, even when looking through a magnifying glass, I could hardly believe that it was in fact made of separate, individual pieces of wood and not painted on to the chest.

Ivan never stops experimenting. He often finds himself reinventing solutions to the kinds of problems which also beset the

original craftsmen. For the marriage chest he had to learn gilding; currently he is exploring medieval painting techniques. He made his first piece of furniture for his own enjoyment, but is delighted to find that his work now gives so much pleasure to others. He has built up a good relationship with the

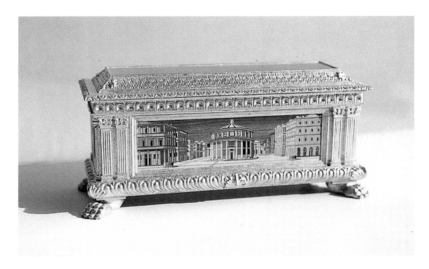

The Italian marriage chest, or *cassone*.

museum curators he has consulted and there have been exhibitions of his work in several museums as well as at the Shakespeare Centre in Stratford-upon-Avon. Ivan also gives talks on the subject, illustrated by a wealth of slides, as well as demonstrations at leading miniatures fairs.

Now in his early seventies, Ivan continues working to build up as representative a collection as possible of early furniture. It took retirement from regular, paid work to provide such a magnificent opportunity to explore the creativity which lay dormant throughout a busy working life, but he is also the first to point out that anyone earning a living as a craftsman would be hard pressed to devote so much time to perfecting each piece. Each of Ivan's miniature masterpieces is the result of up to six months of concentrated effort. Absorbed in his miniature-making, Ivan seems to have found the secret of a happy retirement – work that is pure enjoyment.

Geoffrey Wonnacott

The Cabinetmaker

There was never any doubt that whatever Geoffrey Wonnacott would do as a career, it was going to involve woodwork. He made his first piece at the age of six, nailing together two pieces of wood to make a toy duck, and from then on constructive play (as it is now termed) kept him out of mischief whenever he could get hold of any wood to join together. While still at school, his abilities in the woodwork class were outstanding, and he was also able to get in plenty of practice outside school hours when he took a Saturday job demonstrating woodturning at a Devon crafts shop.

During school holidays he began to help the local carpenter, who was also a wheelwright still practising a skill which is rare even in rural Devon. He enjoyed this even more, as it gave him the opportunity to learn the traditional ways of working, which the old man had learned from his own father. He learned how to make staircases to replace the originals which had crumbled away over the years, as well as cart wheels and even coffins. He was subject to the discipline of doing everything by hand, as the elderly carpenter and cabinetmaker did not believe in using machines.

Geoffrey went on to an apprenticeship as a joiner and then to a regular job with a local firm, where as well as down-to-earth joinery, the work included antique restoration, so that he was able to broaden his knowledge of good quality eighteenth- and nineteenth-century furniture. In his spare time, he made small-scale cabinets for his own enjoyment, and took particular pleasure in constructing the drawers in the same way as the full-size ones in antique pieces. He became proficient at making very small dovetail joints, and there can be as many as 150 dovetails in one of his miniature bureaux today. He also made some small pieces of furniture for his own home, again featuring inlaid work.

Geoffrey first heard about the growing interest in dolls' houses and 1/12 scale miniatures from an article about miniature furniture in a crafts magazine, and when he saw the pictures of the Sheraton-style furniture made by talented craftswoman Margaret Varney he thought he would try this scale. He began by making a Sheraton-style hall table from plans provided by the magazine, and after that first venture into 1/12 scale he subsequently made all his own drawings, based directly on pieces he wanted to miniaturize. He bought an illustrated book on eighteenth-century furniture styles, which included some American furniture, and set to work. His first, award-winning piece was an American colonial chest-on-chest in mahogany. He submitted this for the miniature furniture class at The Woodworker Show in Bristol in 1985 and won a gold medal. His next piece, a Philadelphia highboy made in cherry, also took a gold medal, this time at the larger London Woodworker Show.

By this time it was clear to Geoffrey that his first love was extremely high quality cabinetmaking, not just the joinery he had been trained for. He learned as much as he could about the work of Chippendale, Sheraton and Hepplewhite, and decided that what he really wanted to do was to miniaturize, as accurately as possible, as much of this eighteenth-century furniture as he could. He feels his own work is a tribute to the outstanding craftsmanship of these cabinetmakers, and does not believe in short cuts. He likes to use exactly the same processes as they did and

The Antwerp cabinet. This cabinet on stand dates from the mid-seventeenth century. The miniature is made from ebony and padauk and stands 6¼in (16cm) high. The outer doors have arch panels and pilasters with gilt detail; inside there are 15 dovetailed drawers and a central cupboard which conceals an architectural interior. There are, unusually, 12 tapered ebony legs with ball feet.

feels rewarded for the many hours he spends on fine detail when, in a photograph, one of his own pieces is mistaken for the original.

The main reason he turned to miniature scale, he told me, is that he did not have the opportunity in his regular job to do the fine inlay and decorative painting and lacquerwork which he wanted to try – he couldn't make what he wanted in full size in his spare time because of the cost of the materials, so miniature work seemed a good way round this.

Like many other leading miniaturists Geoffrey prefers to recycle old wood for his miniatures. There is nothing like the best handmade veneers of the past available today, and good quality walnut from a redundant piano can be perfect for his

purpose. Choosing the right wood is vital to the success of the finished miniature. It must be well seasoned and have a good, natural colour, as he does not want to use stain. If you buy modern veneer from a woodshop, it is stacked up so that you can only see the piece on top, he says. In contrast, he can choose just the right grain and colour for each individual piece from his stock and plane it down, ready for use.

Geoffrey checks and rechecks his scale drawings, saying that if anything is wrong on the plan the finished piece will not look right. Everything that might go wrong can be rubbed out on the drawing board, so that when the plans are finished he knows he does not need to worry about errors creeping in. He often works from photographs found

in magazines or books, or pictures sent by customers. As he lives in the middle of Dartmoor, any travel to see an original piece can take valuable time, and if the piece is in America, it is out of the question for him to go and see it.

He finds that his trained woodwork skills enable him to reproduce a piece exactly from a photograph, as he can calculate depth and volume as long as he has one measurement, preferably height, to work from. Many of the pieces which he is asked to reproduce are by famous makers and are well documented. If he checks in several books he can often find photographs taken from a variety of angles and, he says, the more photographs he has, the better.

Geoffrey's outstanding cabinet work shows to advantage on the plainer pieces, such as the William and Mary writing cabinet, where the beautiful figured walnut needs no further adornment. He has also made a speciality of 'japanning', the English cabinetmaker's version of oriental lacquerwork, which became all the rage in the early eighteenth century. An elegant bureau-cabinet with a red, black or green lacquered ground, minutely painted with birds, trees and figures in an anglicized version of oriental motifs, allows Geoffrey to use his artistic ability to the full. He draws the design very simply in pencil on the piece as a guide, but mostly the painting is done freehand, using good quality artist's brushes in a variety of

the smaller sizes (000 is average), depending on the effect he wants to achieve. On the original furniture, he explains, paints and lacquers would have been added in many layers to build up the base for the painted decoration. He uses very thin paints and lacquers which he mixes himself, in exactly the same way, to build up the scaled-down thickness required on his miniature pieces.

Geoffrey says he has to watch the budget agreed with his customer. He can't put in all

the detail he might like to include if he had unlimited time, and didn't have to earn a living. The amount of fine detail required is worked out in advance in discussion with

Right An early eighteenth century William and Mary writing cabinet in beautifully figured walnut with the typical bun feet used at this time. The height is 5¼in (13cm). The cabinet front pulls down to form a writing flap and the interior is fitted with a series of dovetailed drawers; the smallest drawer is ⅞in x ¾in x ¼in (22mm x 18mm x 6mm).

the customer; for instance, he may include parquetry on a piece, but have to leave out the even more time-consuming marquetry if the final result is still to be affordable. But

there is a good side to this: a miniature is often more striking if there is not quite so much fine detail as on the original, as you can see it more clearly.

His tools are the same as those of any woodworker with the exception of specially sharpened chisels to suit the miniscule carving. Where unusual metal handles are called for he will turn them himself, but much of the eighteenth-century furniture used standard brass handles, and these he will buy in from Black Country Miniatures who specialize in accurate 1/12 scale reproductions (*see* page 104). He puts great

emphasis on finishing and finds that the way he works on a polished wood miniature is completely different from how he would deal with a full-size piece. It takes great care and patience to make sure that all the tiny corners have the same finish as the rest of the piece, and he says that hand polishing is essential to achieve the same sort of patina which is to be found on an eighteenth-century original.

Most of Geoffrey's special commissions are to reproduce important historic furniture and the elaborate work on, for example, a piece designed by Robert Adam can take many weeks to complete. But, accepting that a change is as good as a rest, he still finds time to design and make some smaller items for those with a limited budget, and which he can repeat to order. His interest in playing chess as a hobby prompted him to make a replica of his own Staunton chess set: the pieces are individually carved and turned in ebony and boxwood. Astonishingly, as well as the more usual 1/12 scale he also makes the chess set in 1/24. But he does supply some replaceable wax fixing material so that the pieces can be displayed without vanishing if you breathe on them.

Following his early interest in making small boxes he also makes a tiny workbox on stand, elegantly finished

Left A Dutch wardrobe, or *kasten*, a characteristic piece from the New Jersey area of America, made about 1750.

with a burr veneered top and contrasting veneer inside. It stands only 1¾in (4.5cm) tall on gilded paw feet.

Geoffrey's admiration for the work of the great cabinetmakers of the eighteenth century means that he constantly aspires to their levels of perfection. He feels that there is nothing comparable being produced today. The collaboration between Robert Adam as designer and Thomas Chippendale as cabinetmaker was a fusion of talent which occurs rarely, in his opinion.

He visits London and New York only once or twice a year, preferring to stay in Devon and create small masterpieces which will be treasured by their owners and handed on as heirlooms. There are many designers of modern furniture, but very few craftsmen who are capable of reproducing with such skill and precision the exquisite designs of the eighteenth-century masters.

A magnificent Adam sideboard group – the original was made by Chippendale for Harewood House. The miniature is veneered in rosewood and satinwood. The oval inlays are of pearwood, ebony and tulip veneers.

Part Three
Decorative Objects

Gordon Blacklock

The Silversmith

Gordon Blacklock spent his working life as an engineer specializing in metalwork, but it was not until he retired and began a new career as a silversmith that he could make full use of his artistic ability.

At school, Gordon excelled in both art and practical subjects and wanted to go to art school. The need to earn a living meant that instead, he took a five-year apprenticeship in marine engineering, which he could use in his early years in the merchant navy. He then worked for ICI, where he helped to make working models. Before any new plant could be built, a small-scale and then an intermediate version had to be be fully proven. This gave him early experience of working metals in miniature, at that stage in the extremely difficult medium of stainless steel.

Throughout his career in engineering, Gordon continued to paint in oils, to make model aeroplanes in balsawood (as he still does) and to visit historic houses and study their contents. His interest in silversmithing developed after he saw a local exhibition of silver jewellery, and he decided to take an evening course in jewellery-making, where he felt he could combine his artistic ability and experience working with metals.

Gordon sold his jewellery on a part-time basis while still working for ICI, and when he was made redundant he decided to turn to jewellery-making full time. It was then that he first became aware of the demand for miniatures to satisfy the dolls' house market. Told by a friend that he really should go to

Such a miniature piece always appears taller and thinner in proportion than the original if the measurements are scaled down exactly, and adjustments have to be made with great care to compensate for the way in which the eye perceives something very small. Gordon went back to the drawing board and eventually produced a piece which satisfied him – after that, all thoughts of jewellery-making as a full-time career were forgotten. He decided to specialize in Georgian silver because at that time, 1983, the majority of dolls' house collectors favoured this period.

see the work at a local dolls' house fair, he did so. Gordon feels that, wherever possible, miniatures should be made in the same way as full-size pieces, and when he saw some cast miniature silver on display, he

examined it critically and felt he could do better. So he went home and began his career as a silversmith in 1/12 scale.

For his first piece he chose to reproduce a Charles II tankard of around 1670. He made scale drawings based exactly on the measurements of the original and then made a stake (the silversmith's term for a former) from stainless steel so that he could hammer the shape from sheet silver, following the same methods as he used in jewellery-making. He then soldered the body of the tankard on to a base, which he finished with a beaded rim. He shaped the handle from silver wire. It was only when the little tankard was finished ready for polishing that he found that the miniature looked badly proportioned compared to the original.

It was a first lesson in miniature design.

Top **Two candelabra (two-branch with removable central dummy) after J. Schofield, 1795; candlestick after George Ashforth, 1789; chamber candlestick with removable snuffer, George III.**

Above **An oval cake basket, pierced, *circa* 1777; fondant dish with scalloped rim and handle; George I brandy saucepan with ebony handle; and a cake server with fluted edge, hand-engraved, with ebony handle.**

He talks with admiration of the work of the greatest silversmith of the Georgian period, Paul De Lamerie (he himself always spelled his name with the capital D), who was renowned for his magnificent and elaborate commemorative silver. His superb rococo decoration included vines, shells and foliage, scrolls and lion masks, reeding and ribbon work. But it is technically impossible to feature work of this type on small-scale pieces using the original method. *Repoussé* work, as it is called, has to be beaten out from the inside, often followed by further chasing (punching of detail) from the outside. Instead Gordon makes pieces with clean, elegant lines, trelliswork, flat chasing and gadrooning (a decorative pattern of convex curves), setting off the lustre and beauty of the plain surfaces, planished to perfection.

He chooses the pieces he wants to reproduce with great care, after studying the originals in collections or pictured in books. The essential measurement is the height, from which he can work out all the other dimensions to make a working drawing. He buys his sterling silver in flat sheets, solid and hollow rod, and wire of different thicknesses, and uses cast gallery strip in a variety of patterns in fine Britannia silver. Britannia silver is 958 parts pure silver to 42 parts copper, which, being very malleable, is the perfect medium for spinning and for work in which extremely delicate detail must be executed. For spinning, Britannia silver is held in a lathe and rotated at speed and the silver is gently but firmly worked over a hardwood chuck with a steel-headed burnisher until it takes on the exact shape of the chuck.

The more commonly used sterling silver consists of 925 parts pure silver and 75 parts copper, the copper giving the silver a rich colour that only sterling possesses. It is the most versatile of all metals. Although hard and durable enough for its former use in coinage, unlike the softer Britannia silver, it can be forged and drawn like iron and steel, hammered and shaped like copper, cast like bronze and pressed like tin, and is always the first love of the silversmith.

Sterling silver is always hallmarked (unless it is too small to take the mark, like the napkin rings, the salt and pepper shakers and the flatware), and each miniature piece is sent to the London Assay office for this purpose. Where two grades of fine silver, Britannia and sterling, are used in the same piece, the hallmark is for the lower grade (the sterling). Gordon's mark, which incorporates his initials, WGB, is registered at the London Assay office solely for his use

Elegant gadrooned trays – perfect simplicity in miniature.

and appears on each piece followed by a lion (indicating silver), a leopard's head (London office) and a letter of the alphabet for the year of manufacture.

Gordon uses a regular-size engineer's lathe and has to make many of his own tools and stakes. The basic shape for a cake basket, for example, first has to be cut and then soldered into a ring, using a micro-blowtorch. After that, the piece is slipped over a shaped stake held securely in a vice, while it is repeatedly hammered until it is completely smooth and shaped to perfection. Any dents caused during this planishing process finally merge until invisible. When the correct shape has been formed, it is then soldered to the base, after which the handle is fitted. The final process is polishing on a polishing machine which rotates at 2,800rpm. The wheel is rubbed with carborundum for the first polish, and for the second, Gordon uses a minute amount of jeweller's rouge. For a final buffing, he uses a dentist's polishing machine. He says there is no short cut to a perfect finish, just time and patience.

He follows traditional practice in sending pieces to be engraved to a specialist engraver, as was always done by the eighteenth-century silversmiths. Where wooden handles are required, for example on the George I brandy saucepan, he prefers to turn these himself in ebony. The handles are so small that they sometimes shatter or split, so there is some wastage. Precious silver waste, or 'lemel', which accumulates after filing, is carefully saved, though for a miniaturist it can hardly be a vast quantity. 'I'll sell it when I retire,' jokes Gordon.

Gordon finds that the level of concentration required to work on these tiny pieces means that he needs to take a break about every couple of hours, if only to stroll round his garden and admire the vegetables he enjoys growing. Some repetitive shapes are cast in the Britannia silver, such as the bodies for tea and coffee pots, generally in two parts. Gordon handcarves his own master for the mould-maker to work from, and then solders the tiny parts together invisibly. There are four grades of solder available to him – 'hard', 'medium', 'easy' and 'extra easy'. Hard solder has the highest melting point, and so on down the scale. This means that if there are several joints to make, he must start with a harder (higher-temperature) solder and follow on with the others so as not to melt the previous joints. Cast gallery strip in Britannia silver, used on napkin rings and decanter trays, will melt very easily and extreme care has to be used when working with this.

His replica of a George III candlestick with removable snuffer presented Gordon with one of his most difficult problems: the wire used to make the ring around the snuffer is only ⅟₅₀in (0.5mm) thick. Another item where a lot of thought went into the soldering process is a late Georgian toast rack (the original was designed by William Eaton of London in 1836), where there is a total of 23 soldered joints to achieve in a space of

¾in x ½in (18mm x 12mm) without melting each previous joint. This would be impossible to do without a micro-welder and even then demands meticulous precision and great skill.

Silver miniatures have always been specially made for dolls' houses. The dining room of the Uppark baby house, which fortunately survived the terrible fire at Uppark in 1989, contains fine silver tableware which was based on eighteenth-century originals in the full-size house. Much later, the Strong Room in Queen Mary's dolls' house boasts an amazing array of pieces, all reproductions of work from earlier periods.

Today's dolls' house hobbyists are becoming more adventurous and no longer stick rigidly to the Georgian period. Gordon is interested in both Art Nouveau and Art Deco silver, and enjoyed designing and making an elegant Art Deco candelabra and a candlestick with a removable stem so that it can also be used as a flower holder. He has also made, to commission, a replica of a jug and basin designed by Charles Rennie Mackintosh. Gordon went to Helensburgh in Scotland to see the originals in the Hill House, and plans to tackle the Willow Bowl which is on display in the Hunterian Museum and Art Gallery. He hopes eventually to miniaturize several other designs from the early twentieth century, while continuing to reproduce the elegant Georgian silver with which he has made his name.

Art Deco style: two- and four-branch candelabra and a convertible candlestick/flower holder.

Edward Hill
The Glassmaker

Twenty years ago Edward Hill was working in Murano, studying Venetian glassmaking techniques. The glass workshops were originally established in Murano in 1292; successive waves of immigrant workers from the east added their artistic contribution and expertise until, during the Renaissance, Venetian glassware became the most admired in Europe. Edward's work is based on this continuing visual tradition, which has influenced both his working methods and the way he feels about glassmaking in general. He gained a respect for the craftsmen who had worked with glass throughout history, and he began to make a study of historic glass.

Edward worked in Italy for 18 months and the young Italian lady he met at that time is now his wife. When he returned to London he worked for Whitefriars Glass for a few months, to gain experience of production work, which is completely different. At Whitefriars each person is trained to do one job expertly, but not to learn the whole range of skills. Edward soon

Above **A selection of clear and transparent designs of different periods, including Bristol blue and ruby red.**

decided he wanted to set up his own glassmaking workshop, where he could experiment and be in charge of the whole creative process.

He achieved this ambition in 1975 and began making a range of art vases and wine

glasses. While establishing his full-size glassmaking business, he continued to read and visit museum collections, and became more aware of the strong English tradition of glassmaking. This was now even more interesting, because he could understand how each shape had been arrived at. For example, the onion-shaped bottles emblazoned with a seal which were popular between 1650 and 1750 came about because of the way a big-blown gather of glass hangs down from the iron while being made. Gravity causes the future neck of the bottle to thin down, while the onion shape is the result of the base resting on the ground and being flattened while being blown from above. There is always a logical reason for the way in which certain shapes came about.

His first 1/12 scale piece was made after

he saw some small glass ornaments at a craft fair and thought that he could make something both smaller and better. He realized that lampworking (melting rod and tubing over a flame to blow each tiny piece) was the ideal way to achieve this. The techniques that he would use for normal scale glasswork have to be changed considerably for work in miniature. It is not possible to make miniatures from a large crucible of molten glass in a furnace. Instead, he uses glass tubes and rods of various diameters which have been drawn out previously from the furnace and cut into lengths of about 12in (30cm). He heats a small section of these in a needle-size flame produced by an oxy-propane burner.

To make a wine glass, for example, the bowl is blown from a piece of tube. A piece

of glass rod is heated and joined on, then stretched to form a stem. The foot is made from another blown piece of tube which is melted on, then opened out and flared, and finally the top is cut and flame polished to form a lip. Tiny objects have more surface area in proportion to their volume, so another problem with working in miniature scale is that small amounts of hot glass cool much faster than large ones. In fact, according to Edward, the difference between failure and success is often a reviving cup of coffee and having another go.

Edward is now the leading glass blower in the country working in miniature scale, and he produces an astounding variety of period glass, from Roman to Art Deco. He made his first miniature Roman glassware for someone who was creating a dolls'-house-size museum, so that they could display their miniatures in a more formal way than would be possible in a dolls' house. When he studied Roman glass in museums, Edward saw that the bubbles in the glass are always striated in the direction of the flow, showing which way the glass was pulled while being made. When glass is made in a furnace, the reaction of the ingredients creates bubbles which float to the surface of the melt and burst if the glass is very hot and liquid. The primitive furnaces used by the Romans were

Above **Late Georgian ring-neck decanter with twist-stem glass.**

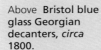

Above **Bristol blue glass Georgian decanters,** *circa* **1800.**

Left **Bubbly glass: Lalique and Marinot,** *circa* **1920.**

not running hot enough for long enough to allow the bubbles to escape. Edward deliberately puts bubbles into all his Roman glass, as well as into glass dating from before 1650. From about that time on, accidental bubbles in glass became rarer because of advances to hotter furnaces.

In the early 1920s the artist Maurice Marinot noticed the beauty of glass which contained bubbles, and he trapped air bubbles deliberately between gathers of hot glass by dimpling the first gather in a mould, or by rolling on chemicals which produced air when covered with a further gather. Edward has imitated some of Marinot's studio glass, where the bubbles are arranged in a disciplined way.

Putting in bubbles is enjoyable, says Edward, but he also relishes the challenge in producing miniature versions of English wine glasses from the Georgian period. English lead crystal was developed during the late seventeenth and early eighteenth centuries and although thicker than Venetian glass, Georgian glass has an astonishing brilliance. However it was a tax on glass by weight, levied in 1745, which brought the development of the lighter air-twist stems. The intricate patterns of white and clear glass are a development of the Venetian technique *vetro a filigrana* which Edward had seen in Murano. Twist stems are begun with furnace work by first covering opal white glass with molten clear glass, then pulling this out into ¼in (5mm) canes, cut up into 6in (15cm) lengths. These are laid out in patterns, and rolled on to a hot cylinder of clear glass. After reheating they are pulled out and twisted by Edward and a helper, walking apart, into lengths of about ⅜in (10mm) diameter. For miniatures, these lengths of cane are then further twisted over the burner flame to take them down to ¹⁄₁₆in (1.5mm) diameter, which still encloses the original white stripes. These stems have between six

133

Victorian gold leaf decanter and vase.

and 16 stripes, and have to be fused on to the bowl of a wine glass very skilfully, as a wisp of flame at 2,000°F (1100°C) will deform thin blown wine glass bowls or fine glass stems instantly. Making matching sets of wine glasses is one of Edward's most difficult tasks when all the work has to be freeblown in this way.

Edward produces a great variety of coloured and lustre glass. Colour is added to glass by using metal oxides, plus other substances which reduce or increase their effect. The strongest oxide colour is blue cobalt, which is mined in the Congo; the usefulness of cobalt in glassmaking was discovered in the eighteenth century and made possible the Bristol blue glass which is still so highly prized today. Strong reds and pinks were difficult to achieve until the Victorians found that they could use gold oxide to make ruby and cranberry glass, which immediately became very popular.

Eventually fashion moved away from the colourful ruby and cranberry glass to the more fluid, sinuous shapes of Art Nouveau.

The Frenchman René Lalique began working as a jewellery designer, but later became so enthusiastic about the potential of glass that he became the foremost designer of moulded glass in Europe. His scent bottles are particularly sought-after by collectors of Art Deco, and Edward makes several miniature versions for the dolls' house collector who admires Lalique's style.

The iridescence on Roman glass as we know it today was caused by the effect of moisture-borne chemical changes taking place while the glass lay in the earth for centuries, developing a silvery patina which is extraordinarily beautiful. Iridescence as an intentional process was much used during the Art Nouveau period, and the acknowledged leader in this field was Louis Comfort Tiffany. The Tiffany studios produced an inventive range of iridesced lustre glass which became immensely popular.

Striking effects can be achieved by iridescing glass, and some of Edward's most spectacular pieces incorporate rolled gold leaf, which is sandwiched between layers of clear glass. As the glass is heated and blown, the gold slowly tears to give an astonishingly beautiful appearance. Although he still does some full-size work, Edward now concentrates almost exclusively on miniatures. And the longer he goes on, the more his artistic appreciation increases. He says he has become far more aware of every minute detail in all sorts of things and finds himself making comparisons between colours, patterns and textures. He finds inspiration for his glass in, for example, the extraordinary variety of delicate colours in a flower petal.

Edward cannot reproduce every style in miniature. He admires the superb crystal made in the late eighteenth and early nineteenth centuries, when each individual maker was able to use his own skills to make inventive designs. The perfection and intricate cutting of some Irish glass, especially Waterford, was renowned for its beauty. But, like lettering on glass, although this would be technically possible in miniature, the time involved would mean that the costs would become exorbitant and beyond the pocket of most collectors.

The most original glassmaking always occurred when the development of a new technique was in its infancy, and the glassmakers were struggling to make it work, Edward says. Innovative styles throughout history resulted in all sorts of colours and ripples, and sometimes odd shapes, and automation has destroyed this rare beauty. In his miniature work he tries to recapture some of the extraordinary variety and magical effect of the best glass from each period, and every time he considers a commission he hopes to create something new and unexpected.

Edward's glass demonstrates his mastery of a wide range of designs and styles.

Michelle Hipkins

Victorian-style Needlepoint

The English woman's traditional leisure pursuit has always been needlework. Fashions come and go, from fine silk embroidery to cross-stitch samplers, from counted thread work to *gros point* on large canvas, and today canvas embroidery is almost as popular as it was during the Victorian era.

Victorian style appeals to dolls' house collectors, and there is a demand for this type of work in miniature scale, so when Michelle Hipkins exhibited at her first fair in 1992, showing finely worked *petit point* designs based on original Victorian charts, worked with up to a staggering 72 stitches to the inch, many miniaturists were delighted.

People were also impressed by the beautiful chosen colours. Most Victorian needlepoint seen today looks muted and drab, so faded from the original shades that we have no conception of their initial effect – and that, of course, is not what we want to

see in a Victorian-style dolls' house, which has been carefully arranged to reflect how it felt when it was new.

Michelle is adept at selecting appropriate colours. The discovery of aniline dyes meant that most Berlin woolwork – the counted cross-stitch designs worked from a chart by the Victorian lady – was overbright, so much so that at first it was a visual shock compared to the work done in the soft, pastel colours permitted by vegetable dyes. Avoiding the extremes, she judges the effect nicely to give a pretty, period effect without the brashness.

There is a second reason for such care: if she were to use the shades suggested in the original charts, and work in such a small scale, a red rose, for example, would look like a blob of red, with no definition or indication of the petals. Her colours will vary from almost a white for the palest shade, to a dark brown, rather than the deepest red indicated in the chart, which would appear overbright. In the finished miniature rose, each petal is clearly delineated, but still with a soft progression of tones. There may be as many as 27 colours used in the design for a footstool top with perhaps three roses and a bud.

Michelle began doing full-scale needlework during a spell in hospital, working a cross-stitch sampler to celebrate the birth of her second daughter. She then went on to produce samplers to her own designs which she sold at craft fairs with great success. She enjoyed the work so much that she soon changed from her initial fine canvas to an even finer silk gauze of 48 stitches to the inch. The finished work could be mounted in jewellery, and this was also something that she could do in the evenings when the children were asleep.

Michelle is lucky in having very keen eyesight. She is able to work on silk gauze with as many as 72 threads to the inch without using a magnifier, or even reading glasses. When working in the evening, however, she takes care to use a daylight simulation bulb. The change of colour that

Opposite **Michelle with some of her work.**

Below **Three gilded footstools: left and right are upholstered in a Victorian floral design sewn on 48-count silk gauze; in the centre is an Empire-style 'griffin and lyre' design, originating from 1810.**

that she went on to work a miniature bell pull in tent stitch. Her mother showed the work to the local dolls' house shop, and the owners immediately suggested that she should do some more. Soon afterwards, Michelle went to a dolls' house and miniatures fair, where she found that no one was selling anything in a similar style to hers, and so the idea of working professionally took root.

Michelle decided to concentrate on Victorian-style needlepoint because she thought it would appeal to many dolls' house enthusiasts. Victoriana is one of her passions, and she loves to read about the furniture and interior decoration of the period. Counted embroidery designs, especially woolwork, had always appealed to her. She already had some nineteenth-century charts for Berlin woolwork, which she had planned to try out, but when she visited an antiques shop which specialized in Victoriana, Michelle had a lucky find which made it possible for her to reproduce many authentic patterns. The

takes place in her silks under normal artificial light could cause costly mistakes.

She was introduced to the dolls' house hobby by her own mother, who was busy furnishing a dolls' house. Michelle decided to make a miniature sampler for it as a birthday present, and her mother was so delighted

bound volumes which she delightedly brought home from the antiques shop were the *Englishwoman's Domestic Magazine*, published in 1868, the *Penny Illustrated Magazine* from 1872, and the French *Journal Moiselles* for 1886. The charts were all printed in vivid colours and were much

The room setting displays a wide range of Michelle's work. The carpet in the centre is based on a design from Persia, sewn on 48-count silk gauze with pure silk threads. It measures 6½in (16.5cm) square and contains 90,000 stitches. On the wall to the left is a wall-hanging, or rug, with six Victorian floral designs. The rug/wall-hanging on the right shows six Victorian animal and floral designs. The picture above the fireplace is of a pastoral scene, popular around 1820, and worked on 48-count silk gauze.

The floral design bell-pull is also 48-count, and has gold-plated solid-silver ends by Ken Palmer.

In front of the fireplace is a hand-turned and carved firescreen, the cat's head worked on 60-count silk gauze.

On the left of the fireplace the tripod firescreen pole has a single rose design, while on the right a Cluny rabbit-design firescreen pole is shown with a matching 1in (25mm) footstool.

The 48-count 'cherub' picture on the easel (left) is based on a tapestry, *circa* 1620, covering a sofa in Burghley House. The ornate square footstool

has handcarved legs and a rose design sewn on 48-count silk gauze.

The oblong and round footstools are mahogany with traditional floral designs.

In the corner there is a handcarved Gothic-style Victorian side chair, with finely turned front legs. In front of this is a second Victorian side chair, made from English walnut with ebony inlay. It too is handcarved and turned, and has a floral design on the seat and back panel, sewn on 40-count silk gauze.

clearer and easier to follow than many modern charts provided by today's designers. She feels that she was especially fortunate to begin just at that time, as antique charts are now very scarce, most already having been snapped up by designers interested in authenticity.

While planning her first appearance at a miniatures fair as an exhibitor, Michelle decided that her work would be much more effectively displayed if it was shown as it might be used in a dolls' house setting. 'What I really need,' she told her husband, Steve, 'is some Victorian-style footstools and firescreens so that I can display the work properly on my stand, perhaps in a room box.' Steve is a sales engineer, although he formerly worked as a machinist and has always enjoyed making models. His only previous experience of woodwork had been trying out his grandfather's old-fashioned lathe – 25 years old and home-made, and which would only run at one speed, but he

These three Victorian chairs are all upholstered with Michelle's needlepoint, which in each case is sewn in silk threads on 48-count gauze. Michelle's husband, Steve, turned and carved the chairs.
Left Oak side chair, upholstered with original Berlin woolwork design.
Centre English walnut side chair, with a Tudor rose design based on a repeat pattern that has been popular over many centuries.
Right Rosewood dining chair with ivy on the back and repeat design on the seat.

agreed to try. His first work – frames for some of Michelle's pictures – was too big, however, and they were told that it must be to scale.

Fred Williams, a member of the Midland Miniaturists Group, specializes in making 1/12 scale frames and was very helpful in advising Steve how to frame Michelle's work. Steve progressed rapidly, and soon decided he needed better equipment if he was to do the job properly. He bought a variable-speed miniature lathe and began to teach himself woodturning. Before long he was producing round footstools, so that they were able to provide a simple display at Miniatura, where Michelle took enough orders to justify continuing. Although there were no stands left available, she was next offered a small display space at the London Dollshouse Festival, only two months later.

Steve now also makes Victorian-style chairs which display Michelle's needlepoint covers to perfection. He likes to use ebony if carved detail is part of the design, and was delighted when he was given some 400-year-old oak by a local builder who had been pulling down some derelict cottages.

Michelle continues to find the old charts a source of inspiration. She had to adapt the designs, extracting elements which will look good on tiny accessories without being too busy. The Victorians often used both *petit point* and *gros point* in the same piece. Working on double-thread canvas, they would stitch the faces and hands of a figure with tiny stitches and fine wool over one thread of the canvas, while the background would be worked in thicker wool in *gros point* over two threads. Besides being effective, they could also complete a large piece of work much faster using this method. Michelle has adapted this idea to work chair backs and footstools, with the central flower design in Swiss handspun pure silk thread, while the background is worked in a soft embroidery cotton.

She uses size 13 or size 15 beading needles, which are the only ones fine enough for her purpose. She works entirely in tent stitch, which gives the neatest effect on the back as well as the front of the work, as it needs to be of an even thickness. She does not favour half cross-stitch as it never produces such a smooth appearance – when finishing, the tiny thread of left-over wool that has to be worked in will make a miniscule ridge.

Michelle is full of encouragement for the rest of us. When I asked her if her work needed stretching into shape, she laughed and said, 'Yes, always.' She prefers to work without a frame and says that as with full-size needlepoint, the piece needs to be blocked and steamed into shape. She follows the usual method of stapling the completed work to a board until it is dry and exactly the right shape.

Once, while steaming a cover for a footstool, the silk gauze lifted and stuck to her iron. She managed to remove it

Below A handcarved and turned black ebony firescreen, with a chinoiserie picture taken from an original Victorian Berlin woolwork chart, *circa* 1830. This is also worked in pure silk threads on 48-count silk gauze.

Bottom The delightful needlepoint versions of the Picasso and Art Deco rugs.

without burning her fingers, but the edges of the gauze were singed badly. It was a lucky escape, as she has to avoid damaging her fingers – when you are sewing for hours at a stretch, using an exceptionally fine needle, the slightest nick will be very painful. Fortunately the work was intact, but she had to trim the gauze much closer to the stitches than she usually does to fit it on to the footstool. Michelle advises people to take heed of her unhappy experience when steaming work into shape, and to use extreme care in handling the work generally. It can still be spoiled when mounting, she cautions – it is all too easy to cut the silk thread of the gauze when trimming.

Michelle likes to produce a new collection for each major miniatures fair, and when she was invited to attend La Fête des Miniatures at the Château de Vendeuvre in 1993, she decided to provide a complete contrast by copying Picasso's *Lady in Red*, and an Art Deco rug for good measure. Both these modernistic designs were snapped up immediately by French art lovers, and she has already been asked for more. At another extreme of popular taste, pictures of Peter Rabbit and Benjamin Bunny are always in demand for the British dolls' house nursery.

But in the main, apart from the many commissions she receives, Michelle will continue to concentrate on the Victorian patterns which are suited to any dolls' house from Victorian style to present day. She still has plenty of antique charts to form the basis of many collections yet to come.

Muriel
Hopwood
Oriental-style Porcelain

Above **Muriel**
painting her
enchanting
porcelain.

Right **Pottery at
various stages of
firing, from
biscuit-fired, to
painted in
preparation for
the next firing.**

Opposite top **The
Arita jar,** *circa*
**1680, boldly
decorated
enamelled ware
made for the
domestic Japanese
market.**

Opposite below
Large platter in
the southern
Chinese provincial
style, known as
Swatow ware. The
designs are freely
executed with
bold brush strokes,
very different from
the contemporary
Ming style.**

If you mention antique Chinese porcelain to potter Muriel Hopwood, her eyes sparkle with enthusiasm. For collectors of miniature ceramics who share that admiration, her name is synonymous with fine craftsmanship – 1/12 scale blue-and-white porcelain based on oriental ware has now become the main part of her output. She was prompted to abandon her previous designs, and begin making replicas of eighteenth-century Chinese porcelain, by the salvage of the Nanking cargo in 1985. More

than 100,000 pieces of Chinese export ware, which had gone to the bottom of the ocean in 1750, were recovered.

Blue-and-white porcelain had been valued in Europe since the first pieces had been brought to Venice by Marco Polo, when its brilliance and translucence caused much astonishment at a time when most Western work was rough and crude by comparison. Early work from the Ming Dynasty was highly prized, and the relatively few pieces which remain in private and public collections mostly have associations with royalty.

When the export ware began to reach Europe in quantity during the eighteenth century it was still considered a status symbol, to be displayed where possible as a complete set of vases known as a *garniture de cheminée*. For the wealthy owner, extra shelves and wall brackets were added around the chimney piece to display as many vases as possible, and it is in reproducing this type of porcelain that Muriel excels. She had already explored a variety of possibilities using her chosen medium, clay, but did not set out to become a potter initially. With A-levels in both art and architecture, she then went on to college in Yorkshire with the idea of qualifying to teach art and also drama.

In her foundation year, when art students have the opportunity to try a variety of disciplines, she began her pottery course. That first experience of firing her beginner's

work in a kiln seemed magical to her. In went this dull, dusty, pinkish shape, and 24 hours later, when it was taken from the kiln, it was transformed into a shiny, slipware pot. She thinks most people who go on to work as potters feel this initial excitement. 'The idea of the four elements – earth, water, fire and air – combining to transform a basic

143

shape into something both useful and ornamental is so simple and pleasing.'

Drama as a subject was abandoned and Muriel went on to teach both art and ceramics, first in Shropshire, and then in Birmingham, where she still lives. Once she discovered her modelling skills, it was almost as though drawing and painting were put on hold while she explored this new world of creativity. She began to make ceramic jewellery in her spare time, which was another way of refining her techniques. Muriel went on to tutor evening classes in ceramic jewellery-making and fitted this in while still teaching at day school.

It was only a short step from making jewellery to dolls' house miniatures. She never felt any desire to make large pots or sculptural forms, but always liked working on small-scale projects. Recognizing the growing interest in dolls' houses as a grown-up hobby, she decided to try 1/12 scale. Her first pieces were terracotta plantpots made from moulds, and she went on to experiment with both red and white earthenware – the basis for traditional English slipware – and a

items. But she realized that there was also a growing demand for more sophisticated tableware and ornaments in appropriate period styles. Much domestic china produced in the Potteries is slip-cast in moulds, biscuit-fired, glaze-fired and then decorated with enamels which are screenprinted in the form of transfers. Another firing at 1470–1530°F (800–830°C) fuses the design into the glaze. Muriel decided to use this method for more elaborate pieces. Her own designs were made into transfers by a local firm, and she began to make decorated bone china tea services.

Next she tried a Victorian plate with piercing around the rim, through which she would thread a fine silk ribbon. She soon had to abandon this design because in the time it took her to thread the ribbon successfully through the minute holes without wastage, she could have made any number of small pots, so that was necessarily a limited edition.

Each new design involved experiment, first achieving the basic shape, making the mould, and then producing the perfect glaze

Muriel's miniature bowl from the Wanli period, *circa* 1580–1600, was inspired by a superb bowl at Burghley House in Lincolnshire. The Burghley House bowl is said to have been a christening gift from Queen Elizabeth I. There are several Wanli bowls in existence, no two alike, and Muriel's version is again slightly different. This fine miniature was a collaboration with Ken Palmer (*see page 161*) who provided the silver mount.

range of kitchenware, such as pudding basins and flan dishes.

Most dolls' house enthusiasts enjoy fitting out a miniature kitchen and she at first concentrated on these simple domestic

for the tiny, fragile pieces. Shrinkage in the kiln – between 10 and 15 per cent is normal – must be taken into account when calculating the proper scaled-down proportions. Mechanical failure has sometimes caused Muriel trouble when firing – her worst experience was when a switch malfunctioned and her kiln failed to switch off. Muriel had stacked four shelves, the result of many hours of work, and when she went to take it out the next day was horrified to find everything still red hot. The glaze on the little pots had vitrified, those on the top shelf had dripped down on to the lower levels and everything had fused together and had to be scrapped. For a long time after that she would only fire one shelf at a time. On another occasion her stand at a miniatures fair was almost bare: she had

chance remark by her husband, Bob, which led her to begin experimenting with the much finer porcelain. Bob shares her interest, and their first visit to the Percival David Foundation of Chinese Art in London was, they both agree, thrilling, and Bob

Above **Imperial yellow Ming dynasty platter and bowls with striking blue, green and red decoration.**

Left **Art Deco – the instantly recognizable style of Clarice Cliff.**

switched on her kiln for a last firing and nothing had happened. Since then she always keeps a spare set of elements in stock so that she can rewire the kiln immediately if necessary.

Muriel's work had progressed from simple earthenware to fine bone china, which was much in demand, but it was a

suggested she really ought to move on to porcelain. Shortly after this came the spectacular finding of the Nanking cargo, and Muriel decided to follow Bob's advice.

She launched her Nanking collection at Miniatura in 1986 and it immediately attracted both public and press attention. From the moment she first heard about the successful salvage, she had begun to explore the possibilities of reproducing some of these pieces in 1/12 scale. She needed to achieve a glaze which would have the beautiful, translucent lustre of eighteenth-century Chinese porcelain, and points out that the background glaze she evolved is not white, but has an intentional grey–blue tinge.

Porcelain is made from a very pure clay which, when fired at high temperature, becomes translucent, unlike earthenware. Muriel's blue-and-white oriental-style ware is painted in underglaze colours made from metal oxides, after an initial, low-temperature firing to harden the clay slightly. It then has a biscuit-firing at 2190°–2230°F (1200–1220°C) which fuses the oxides into the pot, and finally the glaze is added and it is fired again at 2160–2190°F (1180–1200°C).

Although it is not always possible to include the smallest elements of a pattern in such a tiny size, Muriel tries to convey the essence of the design with her delicate brushstrokes. She has come full circle from those early days when her painting seemed unimportant compared to working with clay, and she says it is now the painting which she enjoys the most. No two Chinese pots were ever identical, and Muriel's work is never a direct copy of an original. Instead, she reinterprets each design while following the original artist's intention, in the same way as the Chinese in later centuries expressed their admiration for the work of preceding generations without directly copying. But they, it seems, might carry this as far as including the mark of the original potter, an act of homage which has confused many experts since. All Muriel's pots are signed with her mark, 'H'.

Muriel and Bob are joint organizers of both the English and Scottish Miniatura shows, which takes up a great deal of time, but despite this she continues to explore the world of oriental porcelain. She makes vases in the exquisite *famille rose* style which became highly prized in Europe during the eighteenth century, when pink enamels were introduced into the Chinese palette in response to Western ideas on colour. One of her most difficult tasks is to reproduce bowls with the Imperial yellow ground which was produced in the Imperial kilns. Yellow oxide has a way of making the slip sticky and difficult to work with, Muriel explains, so Imperial ware is very labour-intensive with a high wastage factor. She likes the contrast of this very different colour palette: iron-red and green designs, or a blue dragon, for example.

Left to her own selection of subjects, Muriel might seem content to go on exploring the Chinese and related styles, but a commission may shift her into a completely different mode. One such led her to introduce into her repeatable pieces a number of items based on Wemyss style. This Scottish earthenware, decorated with flamboyant flowers or fruit, became popular in the late Victorian and Edwardian eras and is now highly collectable.

But it was a television programme about the potter Clarice Cliff that inspired her to begin creating Art Deco designs, allowing her to enjoy another contrasting style of painting. The black lines are strong and definite in full-scale, but exquisitely fine when reduced. They have to be applied last, and Muriel has to concentrate very hard in order not to add a fraction too much and spoil the pattern.

Potters throughout the ages have attempted to copy superlative Chinese porcelain, and most studio pottery echoes the basic shapes which were evolved during the fifteenth century. For the foreseeable future, Muriel will continue to create miniature masterpieces which might perhaps receive a nod of approval from those past masters.

A dresser with a selection of Muriel's work.

Carol Lodder
The Potter

Carol Lodder is a gifted studio potter whose skills in both throwing and hand-painting in the miniature scale are formidable. Her work is based firmly on the English tradition established in the seventeenth century, which includes elements taken from earlier oriental pottery. She is not a copyist but, instead, reinterprets shapes and patterns which have themselves evolved from early Chinese and Japanese porcelain. English seventeenth- and eighteenth-century pottery and porcelain used the same decorative motifs in new ways. The peony flower, for example, which had been used on fifteenth-century Chinese porcelain, reappeared on English delftware, but adapted and anglicized.

Carol's enthusiasm is contagious, but she did not set out to be a potter. After a foundation year at art college she intended to go on to the degree course in fashion design. However, while studying plaster-casting as part of the general course, Carol found she had an instinctive feeling for the clay and that she enjoyed producing three-dimensional objects. It was clear that her modelling skills were well above average, so she decided to abandon fashion studies in favour of a degree course in ceramics. It was the throwing that appealed to her most, the element of risk, the feeling of never knowing what was going to happen, and for her, throwing is still the most exciting part of making pots.

She went on to work in potteries in Scotland and Devon, getting plenty of practical experience, and also taught in summer school in Herefordshire for several years. This was really useful, she says, because there is nothing like being asked a question you have to answer immediately to concentrate the mind. It makes you think hard about the way you yourself work, to analyse the basic shape you start with to make an open form like a bowl or an elongated one like a bottle, in order to describe to the

student what they, in turn, should do.

The need to be a fund of knowledge about pattern and design when teaching encouraged Carol to visit museums, to look and learn. She says the ceramics collection in the Victoria & Albert Museum is so inspirational that she returned again and again – and still does. She soon realized that the pots which appealed to her most were those handmade by craftsmen in small workshops or factories, before the advent of industrialization. She loves unsophisticated Staffordshire slipware, rough peasant pottery and delftware, on which you can see the

workshop. The chimney pots were missing and Carol's mother suggested she should throw some new ones, copying them from the chimney pots that, for safety, had recently been taken down from their own cottage. Carol nearly gave up in frustration, but after a whole day's work she had produced a large pile of soggy disasters – and two good chimney pots, some flower pots and, for good measure, a casserole dish. At this point, she became hooked on throwing small pots. It was, of course, triumphing over the difficulties which appealed. When working in 1/12 scale, she says, 12 times the

individual brush strokes of the painter.

This growing familiarity with pottery and porcelain from many periods and countries meant that when she finally began to make miniature pots, Carol knew what she wanted to achieve. However, when she set up her own pottery in the Dorset countryside in 1981 she began by making full-size tableware, which she sold at local craft fairs. She made a few miniatures too, for fun – although not as yet 1/12 – and found they sold just as well as her full-size pots.

Her first attempt at an even smaller scale came while renovating the family dolls' house, which had resurfaced when the garden shed was converted into her

care is needed. There is no place for sloppy craftsmanship, and even blowing away a bit of fluff can have disastrous results, because feather-light pots may fly away and splatter on the floor. This early lesson was learned one day when, without thinking, she did just that – and lost a whole row of pots which she had set out to dry.

Despite the problems, Carol continued throwing rather than using moulds because she wanted to make each pot individual. She had chosen quite a fine clay for her full-size pottery, which she was also able to use when she tried her first stoneware miniatures, allowing her to put them in the kiln around the larger stoneware pots at the same firing

Above **Two Imari jars and two in blue-and-white ware.**

Opposite top **A blue dash charger.**

Opposite centre **Blue dash chargers, depicting traditional subjects: Adam and Eve, and the Green Man.**

Opposite bottom **A large punchbowl with lettering, and Fazackerley Flowers vase and jug.**

temperature. An experiment with glazing led to her making the brown and cream stoneware cider jars and hot water bottles familiar in the West Country, and she then expanded into a whole range of old-fashioned stoneware miniatures.

Customers at craft fairs told her that there was bound to be a demand for such pieces from dolls' house collectors. She decided to increase her miniature work, as she now felt ready to try something a little less rustic than the country-style stoneware. One of the main turning points was an exhibition of embroidery at a local manor house. When she looked at the beautiful English flowers embroidered in colourful silks, she felt she would like to paint something similar on her pottery. She searched out a fine, white clay that she could use specifically for miniatures, and this opened up for her a whole new world of colour decoration. Carol prepares her clay with great care, starting out with about 2lbs (1kg) to knead. Quite a lot of it ends up in the water-filled wheel tray when throwing, and this can be recycled and used again. She has to be careful, however, not to gather up any impurities at the same time, as it is important that there is no grit in the clay – the tiniest piece of grit on the thin, spinning edge of a 1/12-size pot behaves like a small rock hurtling around the rim of its full-size counterpart. 'One blink and a pot just isn't there any more,' Carol told me.

Learning how to create each new shape requires practice and perseverance. There is such a tiny amount of clay on the wheel that it gets waterlogged very quickly, so the shaping stage has to be done fast. Each time she tries a new shape, she is continually experimenting until she has mastered it.

Carol uses books for research, and was attracted by a picture of an English delftware mug produced by Thomas Fazackerley in 1757. She could not go to look at the original piece, which had been destroyed in

151

the Second World War when it was housed in Liverpool Museum, but even though the picture she referred to was black and white, she had by now become so familiar with the colours used by the different English

A Japanese Kakiemon ware porcelain bottle, two tea bowls and two jars.

(3mm) long. These wear rapidly on the rough, biscuit-fired surface and have to be repeatedly trimmed to shape. Different brushes are used to paint lines of various thicknesses, but size 10/0 is typical. The first

factories in the eighteenth century that she found she was able to visualize how it would have looked. At that time potters had to grind and mix all their own pigments, and colours were limited to those that could be made from the raw materials available. The Fazackerley palette included black, yellow, red, blue, green and lilac. Carol feels fortunate that she can now go to a supplier and find a tube of almost any colour that she needs, to copy those which the seventeenth- and eighteenth-century potters produced from their basic metal-oxide pigments.

Her enthusiasm for the Fazackerley pattern resulted in a range of pieces. The design of delicate flowers has to be altered subtly to suit each shape, curving round on a bowl or elongated very slightly on a large serving dish. The correct glaze is crucial when the work is to be decorated. There are infinitesimal variations in how the colour will appear on a specific glaze, and if the brush strokes are too thick the paint may run.

She uses very fine brushes less than ⅛in

firing before painting leaves the pots in a very fragile 'biscuit' state. They have to be handled with great care and, Carol says, it is rather like painting on blotting paper. Inevitably she loses some as they disintegrate.

Fazackerley Flowers is only one pattern in a whole range of English delftware which Carol makes. Dutch delftware was superior to English as the Dutch potters were more advanced and went on to develop more detailed decoration, often using enamels, which was not attempted in England. However, it is the somewhat rustic image which appeals to Carol in the English delftware – the adaptation of a Dutch design which had already been adapted from a Chinese original.

If she were asked to make a replica of a full-size delftware bowl, Carol says she would feel constrained to copy it exactly. She actually prefers to interpret designs freely, so that each piece she paints is unique. Her large plates, or chargers, are some of the most time-consuming, and are only made for special shows or to commission. The seventeenth-century originals, often dated, were painted in an amusingly naive way, sometimes depicting a royal personage in an almost cartoon-like image, or a biblical subject such as Adam and Eve. It takes an entire afternoon to paint one of these subjects in minute detail and Carol has to be in exactly the right frame of mind to do it successfully. Recreating something which was once in regular domestic use appeals to Carol: a punchbowl where she can add lettering is one example; another is an English puzzle jug with both piercing and lettering.

Although she favours throwing, Carol does use moulds to make square-edged flower bricks and decorative seventeenth-century shoes, with square toes and bows, which would be impossible to throw on a wheel. The tiny bows for the shoes are made separately in an even smaller mould and then attached. The original shoes were made in the Lambeth pottery in 1688, purely as ornaments. It is thought that the flower bricks were used to hold lavender or potpourri, not cut flowers, as there is no trace of water having been used in any of those which survive in museums. Each of her miniature moulds can be used only a few times before Carol has to make a new one, as they wear out quickly and, if overused, would turn out inferior pots.

Carol's work continues to evolve. As well as the traditional English pottery for which she has become well known, she is now making porcelain, and finds the colourful Japanese Kakiemon ware inspiring. Kakiemon ware was developed in the late seventeenth century primarily for export to the West. It was so much admired that by

Carol made her room setting – based on Charleston farmhouse in Sussex, home of artists Vanessa and Clive Bell and Duncan Grant – for a special exhibition to display her versions of their studio pottery.

the 1750s both the Worcester and Chelsea factories were making, not exact copies, but free adaptations of the style. As a contrast to the delicate palette of her other work, Carol enjoys using the brilliant enamels and gold so characteristic of the best of Kakiemon ware. She has to remind herself not to be too self-indulgent and spend an entire afternoon decorating just one piece, but it is the opportunity for free expression in a continuing tradition which allows full rein to her creative talent.

153

Alan McKirdy
The Early Music Specialist

To restore keyboard instruments for a living is unusual enough, but to make replicas of them in 1/12 scale is even rarer. Alan McKirdy works at both careers simultaneously. His skills as a restorer are much in demand in the Long Melford area of Suffolk, where he lives and works, but he finds miniature-making equally absorbing.

Alan started in the antiques business after leaving the army, when he began restoring furniture. His only training for this was woodwork at school, pursued with such single-mindedness that he eventually persuaded the headmaster of his highly academic school to allow him to include it in his final examinations, and he was awarded a distinction. He intended to train as an architect but the war put a stop to that plan. He also learned to play a variety of instruments for pleasure. Initially he wanted to try the organ, but was told he must first learn the piano. Then he acquired a battered violin which he managed to repair himself. Years later, he mastered the cello and in the end also became an accomplished organist. His great love is early chamber music.

In the restoration trade he learned a lot about antique furniture, and the day the dealers he worked for acquired a Victorian piano made for a child to play, he began to learn about musical instruments. The piano was exceptionally small: the keys were almost complete, but the action was wrecked and he was asked if he could repair it. He did so by first taking it apart to find out what needed to be done – and finished with it in perfect working order.

Eventually, Alan was able to establish his own workshop, and began to combine restoring general antiques with work on whatever musical instruments came his way. His first attempt at making something in miniature scale came about when friends asked if he would be willing to try to make a

154

1/12 scale pole screen, so that *petit point* could be mounted in it for display in a dolls' house. Alan liked the idea and agreed. He already had a stock of finest-quality Cuban mahogany which he had bought from a timber yard that was closing down. It was sawn in 1897, and had been kept in stack, so it was well seasoned. This was the ideal – and now generally unobtainable – wood for miniatures. Cuban mahogany had always been the most highly prized, which sadly accounted for its near extinction. The two elegant pole screens he produced had springs concealed inside the brass mountings attaching the screens to the poles, so that they could be adjusted in height, just like the eighteenth-century originals he copied.

His next miniature piece was a tilt-top table, followed by a more ambitious Regency dining table. This time he found he needed to make something else that moved, too. The original table had the rolling brass castors which make an elegant finish to much Regency furniture, so Alan experimented until he had produced working castors. These were machined out of solid brass, using the small precision-engineering lathe he had bought when setting up his workshop. He found he had a certain instinct for metalwork and puts this down to heredity: both of his great-grandfathers were machine engineers. His friends, delighted with the miniatures he made for the dolls' house, were keen for him to continue to make in this scale, and he

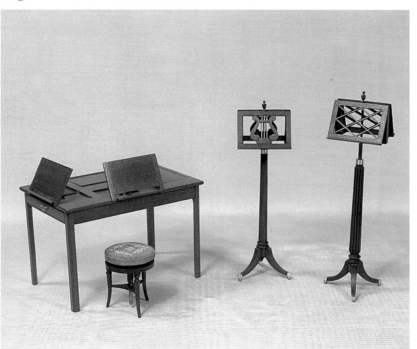

Opposite
Alan McKirdy marking out the string positions on the bridges of a grand piano.

Above **Quartet table in mahogany shown with two desks open and two closed. The two adjustable music stands are of slightly differing design. All three pieces are typical of the late eighteenth century. The height of the tripod stool can be adjusted.**

visited several miniatures fairs with them.

By this time full-size work was starting to quieten down as the recession began to take hold, so for the first time, Alan began to consider making more than just the occasional miniature. He decided to make a start on reproducing musical instruments, and he already had a model to copy – a square piano he had acquired in 1949 which he was going to restore himself. 'I had to buy it,' he said, 'because the owner was going to sell it to someone who wanted to convert it into a dressing table, and I couldn't let that happen.'

First he made accurate drawings of the full-size instrument, to scale down. Next he made a template for the entire soundboard layout. This includes the pins to which the strings are attached. There is a set of fixed 'hitch' pins at one end and 'wrest' pins (used to tune the strings) at the other. On the real instruments these rotate, but on the model they are fixed. The template also indicates the shape and position of the bridges and the exact position of all the strings. The whole soundboard assembly is polished and strung up, after which it is glued to the baseboard and then the case sections are glued on. On the square piano the keyboards had to be fitted before the stringing, as the action, which is attached to the keys, extends beneath the strings. (For his later harpsichords, the keyboard could be fitted after the stringing).

For the full-size instruments, similar methods of construction (and the variants of them that are found in other, related instruments) have continued for about 200 years and have often led to problems. Early instruments were lightly strung, using relatively soft wire, but as they got more sophisticated and stronger wire was used, the resulting tension often caused the cases to buckle. 'If you look at a harpsichord made after 1786,' Alan told me, 'you will generally

Square piano in mahogany with ebony stringing (John Broadwood & Sons, London, 1820).

assembly began to distort. So he slackened off the tension, straightened it out, then thinned the soundboard to just $\frac{1}{16}$in (1.5mm) thick. He then fixed a $\frac{1}{8}$in (3mm) thick steel reinforcing plate very firmly to the back of it, and covered that with another thin layer of wood to bring it back to its original thickness of $\frac{1}{4}$in(6mm) – the full size equivalent is 3in (76mm) thick. He then retensioned the strings and as it remained stable, he fitted the case and all was well. At this point, he found

find that the case is slightly out of true. The use of stronger wire meant that the stringing could have much greater tension.'

So Alan was faced with a difficult problem. What wire should he use for the strings? The finest steel wire he could get was standard music wire, made of hard steel, and when he tried it out his tiny soundboard

someone who was willing to draw very fine, soft iron wire which was historically correct, to replace the modern steel. The thinnest iron wire that could be made was $\frac{4.5}{1000}$in (0.011mm), which was still a little over scale but looked right, and this soft wire could be tensioned without putting undue strain on the case.

Although they may no longer be necessary for strength, Alan still fits steel plates in the baseboards of his instruments, now mainly because people tell him, without knowing the reason, that his instruments feel solid and substantial (*see* page 83). So although they are now there primarily as ballast, they do give an absolute guarantee against any possible future distortion. The only model where this is unnecessary is the walnut spinet. Even in full size these are very

Early-eighteenth-century spinet in walnut (Thomas Hitchcock, London) and walnut stool with bargello embroidery by Michelle Hipkins (*see* page 136). The spinet is the only instrument which does not have a steel plate fitted to the baseboard.

did not find any insuperable problems. His flair for metalwork enabled him to design hinges so that the lids can be folded back in exactly the same way as the originals. He uses sheet brass $\frac{1}{100}$in (0.25mm) thick, which he rolls and cuts to make five knuckles that are then threaded through with the finest wire. The elaborate decorative hinges on the harpsichords are photoetched to his design by Black Country Miniatures. After photoetching these have to be rolled and cut

light-weight instruments and as they have a large overhang to the right of the legs, additional weight would probably make them top-heavy.

A lot of thought and care went into making the cases, but with his trained cabinetmaking skills and extensive knowledge of this type of instrument, Alan

to form the knuckles in the same way as the plain butt hinges.

For the keys he recycles old ivory and ebony piano keys (*see* page 87) of which there are plenty left over from his full-size restorations. In general, the front ends of the old ivory keys are damaged, but the parts which lay between the ebony keys are

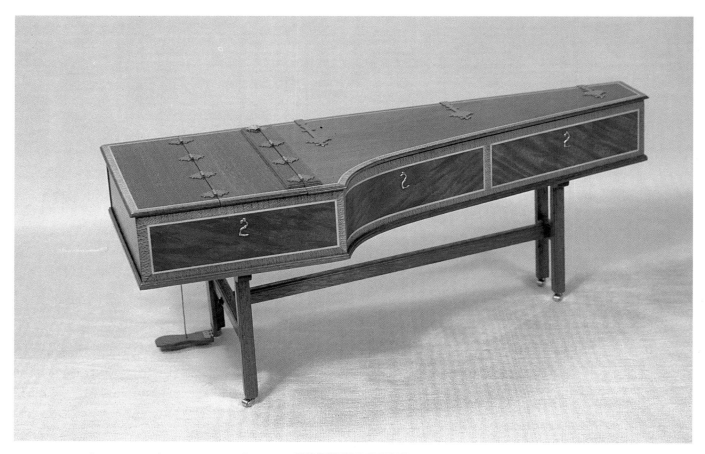

unworn, so he reuses that section. The miniature ebony keys have a square section which is only ½₅in (1mm) and he needs to use the straightest, finest grain of ebony for this, so sometimes he uses new wood if none of his old keys are suitable. The keyboard is made of pearwood with a boxwood facing glued to the front edge. It is then planed to exact thickness.

The covering for the naturals (on a standard keyboard, the white keys) is then glued on. Here there is a fundamental difference from the full-size instrument, which has separate keys: in the miniature they are fixed, so a cover can run along the top of them in one or several pieces, taking care to ensure that any joint comes in the proper place between two keys. This covering is then levelled off, sanded and given a preliminary polish. Using a saw only ³⁄₁₀₀₀in (0.075mm) thick, the next stage is to

Above
Double-manual harpischord in mahogany with harewood crossbanding, shown closed to display hinges (Shudi and Broadwood, London, 1782).

Opposite **The chamber organ (attributed to George England, London, *circa* 1780).**

cut the grooves to suggest separate keys. After cleaning up the saw cuts and a final polish, the sharps (normally the black keys) are spaced along the keyboard using a specially designed jig, and glued in place.

A common question at miniatures fairs is, 'Can you play it?' The answer is 'no', none of Alan's musical instruments produce any sound. He passes the wires down through the wrest pin holes and then drives the pins in to secure them. This means that the strings are not tunable. Alan says that although it would be possible, theoretically, for him to make the instruments tunable, because of the length of the scaled-down strings, at least half of any notes produced would be inaudible – except perhaps to a bat! And for the notes that are still within the range of human hearing, a steel-reinforced 'sounding board' will do nothing to reinforce them.

After tackling the square piano, single- and double-manual harpsichords and a spinet, Alan decided that it was time to make a chamber organ. Some years before, he had restored a chamber organ acquired at a local auction and, as always, had kept detailed notes and measurements. The miniature chamber organ in his catalogue is the result of his attempt.

Early strung keyboard instrument cases are really a specialized branch of cabinetmaking, but an organ case is high-class joinery – everything slots together with mortise-and-tenon joints. This particular instrument is dated 1823, but as organ building was highly conservative, similar chamber organs were made from about 1780 onwards. It is a very neat instrument: the keyboard slides in and the candle brackets also swing in to enable the hinged flap to be closed. The pipes on view over the keyboard are accurately carved and finished in 23ct goldleaf. Alan says that many people do not realize that these pipes on a chamber organ are dummies, usually made in wood. The reason is that in a domestic chamber organ it would cause a gross imbalance of sound for the audience if some of the pipes were in front and some inside. Also, it would be almost impossible to tune the front pipes, because you have to tune them from the back.

159

Ken Palmer
Automata

Above **Ken Palmer**
at his workbench.

Right **A table clock
from the time of
Charles II.** Thomas
Tompion is the
best-known maker
of English clocks in
this period, but
there were several
other fine makers
at work, all
producing clocks
with veneered
ebony cases and
chased and
mercurial gilt
mounts. The dial
on Ken's clock is in
etched brass.

Opposite
Ken's longcase
clock, showing the
working pendulum
which took so
much time and
patience to
achieve.

en Palmer likes to know
how things work, and then
to develop his own ways of
producing working models
in miniature. As a small
child, he would take apart any mechanical
toy he was given to find out what made it
move along or produce a sound. This did not
make him popular with his relatives at the
time. However, it was this streak of curiosity
about mechanical objects which eventually
led him to become a maker of 1/12 scale
automata and working clocks, both rarities
in the dolls' house world.

A dictionary definition of an automaton
reads 'a piece of mechanism having its
motive power so concealed that it appears to
move spontaneously'. The example given is
'clockwork mice'. Although we may not want
to have clockwork mice in our dolls' houses,
a working clock or musical box is an
attractive idea. And a grown-up 'toy' will give
as much pleasure as those full-size marvels
which were such a source of amazement and
delight in the eighteenth and nineteenth
centuries.

Originally, Ken had no idea that he
would enter this esoteric world, although he
did know he wanted to do something
practical, and which he hoped would
combine his mechanical bent with his strong
artistic talent. During his schooldays he had
tried out all sorts of ideas in the garden shed,
and again made himself unpopular with the

grown-ups when he made gunpowder and succeeded in shooting ballbearings across the garden. Later, and more usefully, he learned to use an old treadle lathe. After school he trained at the Birmingham College of Arts and Crafts to become a woodwork teacher. He excelled at cabinetmaking and also managed to fit in a year's course in silversmithing.

Ken went on to teach 11- to 18-year olds, eventually becoming head of his department at school. He enjoyed teaching, as well as a variety of other things – one of his interests is photography – and he is a Fellow of the Royal Photographic Society. The silversmithing was another craft which he could pursue alongside his teaching career. He joined the West Midlands Craft Guild, and exhibited his jewellery designs, which were set with semi-precious stones such as malachite, turquoise and agate, so that the hobby would not become too expensive to pursue. Even so, he gained a reputation for his workmanship that led to many special commissions.

He became interested in dolls' house miniatures when he saw the 1/12 scale porcelain produced by a teaching colleague, the potter Muriel Hopwood (*see* page 144). He decided to try out some ideas of his own, and became so enthusiastic about this new outlet for his silversmithing skills that eventually the full-size jewellery-making had to be discontinued, to give him enough time to concentrate on the miniatures. Ken says now that he feels his earliest efforts were variable

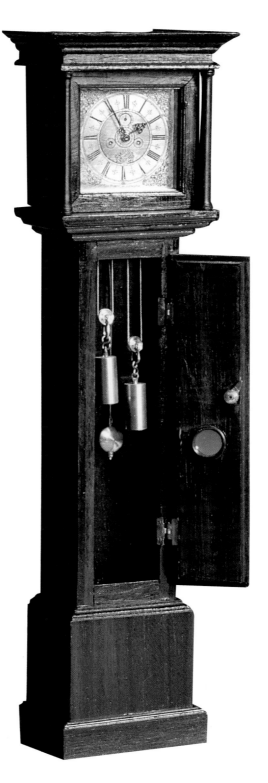

in both scale and quality, but when he was asked if he would like to demonstrate silversmithing techniques at the first Miniatura dolls' house and miniatures fair, he was happy to oblige. He enjoyed the reactions of people watching his demonstrations, as he made simple items such as punchbowls and ladles, but had not expected that anyone would want to buy his demonstration pieces. But they did, and he soon found himself with a list of orders to complete.

Ken's now extensive range of silver is deservedly popular, but he was never content with just one outlet for his talents for long – he wanted to make something for the dolls' house which would work. He thought how nice it would be to have a tiny working clock, so that when people opened the dolls' house they would be able to tell the time. He decided on a late-seventeenth-century table clock, because in that period English clocks were considered to be the best in Europe, and the classic designs are visually appealing. It meant that he could use both his woodworking skills to make the elaborate and beautiful case in ebony, and then his silversmithing for the pierced brass basket top.

He knew quite a lot about clock mechanisms, having predictably, over the years, taken to pieces clocks and watches of all descriptions. The problem was to produce something which could be fitted inside a clock that would be only 1¾in (4.5cm) high. With regret, he abandoned the idea of making an entire traditional clockwork mechanism himself, as he didn't think that anyone would want to wind up a miniature clock every day. Instead he settled for a modern quartz-regulated watch movement which would need to have the battery changed only once in two years.

He made the dial and the hands. A watch dial never looks right when used in a miniature clock because clock figures in full size are cast and are three-dimensional, whereas most watches have plainer figures or just index lines. The miniature hands, too, need to be more elaborate than those of a watch, and have a decorative scroll on the hour hand.

Delighted with the success of his table clock, Ken went on to make a longcase clock with a working pendulum, a project which was full of problems for him to solve. It is not accurate in one respect – he points out that the pendulum swings faster than in a full-size clock with a pendulum perhaps 3ft (1m) long. But the faster swing, caused by the tiny size, actually does look right on a miniature.

Even before he made his first miniature working clock, Ken had been thinking about an even more adventurous project. He feels that the serious collector should be able to have everything in their dolls' house that they might have in their home, and one particularly delightful object which he remembered from his own childhood was a singing bird automaton which could be made to perform on demand. His great aunt would wind the mechanism and run it as a special treat when he visited her. He has studied automata for years, fascinated by the way in which an elaborate system of cogs,

The first singing bird automaton was patented in 1861 by Blaise Bontems in France. Ken's bird is just waiting to be set in motion when offered some bird seed – the concealed switch is activated by a magnet. Ken enjoys demonstrating his singing bird – people look so astonished and delighted to see it working.

cams and levers can be meshed together so that with one turn a whole sequence of movements can be set off.

In the eighteenth century some of the first makers of automata were members of prestigious scientific bodies in both England and France, and many of their plans and designs are still on record. These ideas were developed to be demonstrated to the public, often by clockmakers, who have their own much longer traditions of mechanisms that swing out figures that perform as the clock strikes.

Ken's idea was to produce something tiny but appealing, and remembering the little bird in its golden cage, he thought this would be ideal. But first he had to find a way of disguising a mechanism which would be too large to be concealed in the base of a delicate cage only 1⅛in (30mm) high. The movements of the bird, which flutters its wings and opens and closes its beak as though singing, are activated by a set of cams; a further cam works a circular bellows and yet another moves the plunger of a tiny swannee whistle which emits rapid twittering sounds of variable pitch, warbling so fast that they resemble bird song. The golden cage is fixed to the top of either a 1/12 scale display table or a chest of drawers, which Ken makes to hide the drive and birdsong mechanism.

Since perfecting his singing bird, Ken has gone on to make other miniature automata, all limited editions which are signed and dated, and says that each one sets him different problems. An endearing rabbit which pops up from beneath a lettuce, accompanied by music, proved even more complicated than the bird, necessitating the production of three minute wooden cams which are attached to a musical box movement, and which lift the lettuce 'lid' and make the rabbit pop up.

Ken also continues to make a wide variety of outstanding silver miniatures, discontinuing items from time to time so that he can enjoy the challenge of making something new. He did come to grief on one occasion, when he borrowed a trombone from a friend to photograph as reference for a new model. The trombone arrived in its case ready to be assembled by the musician in the normal way. Having done this, Ken took the photographs he would use as reference and then returned the instrument

Above **Ken's delightful rabbit-with- lettuce automaton.**

Below **A carousel musical box for the dolls' house nursery.**

to its owner. He made six silver trombones which all sold successfully – until the last was bought by a gentleman who had a large collection of full-size musical instruments. The next day, Ken had a telephone call pointing out that his miniature trombone would be ideal for a left-handed trombonist, and it was only then that he realized he had put the slide on the wrong side. The miniature was returned for alteration and soon put right – but Ken says there are still five people out there somewhere who have, and doubtless cherish, what might appear to be a left-handed trombone.

For the future he would like to concentrate more on limited editions and commissions as well as his general range of miniatures. He finds that the challenge of making such special items satisfies his urge to create something new and different. He was especially delighted to be asked to make a two-handled lidded bowl based on one designed by Charles Robert Ashbee, as the Arts and Crafts period is one of his great enthusiasms, appropriately enough for someone who first qualified at a college of arts and crafts. In this case there was an additional reason for his pleasure, as this piece was intended as a gift to the organizer of Miniatura, Muriel Hopwood (*see* page 142), who had originally encouraged him to try 1/12 scale.

Tim Sheppard
The Bibliographical

T im Sheppard took over Lilliput Press, Bristol, as a going concern in 1990. After working at a variety of jobs, he had finally decided that miniature book publishing was what he really wanted to do as a career, and since then he has shown total commitment. Allan Armstrong had founded Lilliput Press in 1984, after many years specializing in the restoration of antiquarian books. The miniature books had become so successful that he had difficulty in keeping pace with orders, and really needed some help.

Tim agreed to give him a hand, initially just for a short time, but found the work so absorbing that, although never an official apprentice, he worked for Allan for almost four years, on and off, learning everything he could. He had always been dextrous and enjoyed the precise work, without any thought that it might become his permanent career.

However, by 1989 Tim was beginning to realize that his future probably did lie in publishing, and he took a City and Guilds

course in desktop publishing and graphic design. Shortly afterwards Allan found that due to a combination of eye trouble and an increasing commitment to his contemporary art gallery, he was no longer able to continue with his miniature books. The result was that Tim relaunched Lilliput Press.

To a collector, or 'micro-bibliophile', the definition of a miniature book is that it must measure less than 3in (7.6cm) in height. Such books have been produced since the fifteenth century and grew in popularity in times of religious persecution when they could be concealed easily.

Miniature books for dolls' houses are a more recent development, and the best-known collection in Britain is in the library of Queen Mary's dolls' house at Windsor

Castle. These are all real books, finely bound, some of which contain original, handwritten stories by a leading author of the day. These include Sir Arthur Conan Doyle, W. Somerset Maugham and Walter de la Mare. Rudyard Kipling wrote out and illustrated in miniature several of his own poems. The library also contains some printed books, of which the miniature atlas, published as a limited edition by Edward Stanford, cartographers to the king, in 1928, is perhaps the rarest.

Few historic dolls' houses have real books. In most cases the books are simulated in the same manner as the many fake books in libraries designed and fitted out by Robert Adam. Dolls' house owners nowadays often simulate books in a similar manner, but on close examination it is easy to see the difference from a properly bound book.

The problems in printing and binding books in a size which is suitable for today's dolls' house collector, where house and contents are all 1/12 scale, are formidable. Given the standards of the Miniature Book Society – the 3in (7.6cm) height limit – Tim's work is a *tour de force*. The leather-bound, hand-tooled and gilded limited editions are 1⅓in (34mm) high, and highly sought-after – by both specialist collectors of miniature books, and dolls' house owners who want fine books to display as individual volumes on a desk or table or in the dolls' house library. For the general dolls' house market, Tim produces books measuring no more than 1in tall x ¾in (25mm x 19mm) wide, which are still legibly printed even in this small size, and are case-bound in Indian silk.

All books published by Lilliput Press are

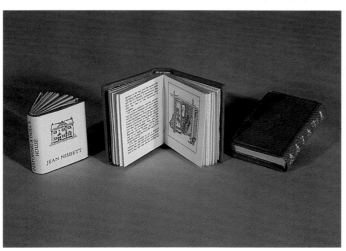

Jean Nisbett's miniature book *Restoring a Dolls' House*, in a smaller version for the dolls' house, and a luxury leather-bound edition.

illustrated, each picture being first drawn by an artist in a large size and then reduced in stages. After the text and pictures have been printed, each illustration is hand-coloured before it is bound into the book. In the limited editions all the pictures are in colour. In the dolls' house version, to keep costs down, only the frontispiece and dust wrapper are hand-coloured, with the pictures inside printed black and white.

The hand-painting is just one process in many. Tim's work begins with the choice of book. A lot of thought goes into this – about the suitability of a particular text, and whether the illustrations will be clear and attractive when much reduced in size. Like any other publisher, he needs to bring out new editions and commission new work. The sculptor Paul Mount has specially written a children's story in verse, entitled *Abdul the Wise*, for Lilliput Press. The unusual illustrations were provided by the young girl for whom he wrote the stories. By contrast, in the same year Lilliput Press brought out *The Age of Chivalry*. This is an account of knights of old, their training and moral code, and the extraordinarily detailed illustrations are taken from fifteenth-century originals.

The text may need to be shortened, while remaining coherent and interesting, in order to fit on to the maximum number of pages possible in such a small book. The average number of pages is 54 and this is governed by the thickness of the paper. Tim uses the best quality bond paper of the minimum usable thickness. One of the limitations is that the paper must be thick enough to take hand painting without the paint going straight through. The paper must also be suitable for printing by the offset litho process, which will provide both clarity and legibility even in this very small size. To ensure that his very high standards are maintained, Tim does all his own design and typesetting on a powerful computer. Eventually he wants to have complete control over not only the design and typesetting, but also the next – film – stage, which at the moment he has to have done for him.

Tim displays some of the beautiful illustrations from *The Age of Chivalry*.

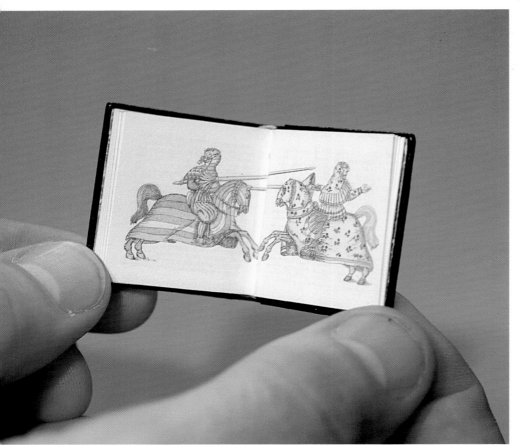

He continues to work with the same printers used by his predecessor. For miniature work, their greatest single problem is registration: few printers are able to maintain their machines in a fine enough condition to work within such tolerances, while at the same time doing other, full-size work. Pete and Heather Jeffery of Bristol have very high standards and regard the printing of miniature books as an art form in

itself. The printed spreads are then returned to Tim for binding.

Hand-binding a book by traditional methods involves 19 different processes, and some of these involve a number of separate stages. There are no short cuts. Few people realize just how much care and skill has gone into producing one of these tiny volumes. The tools used are fairly simple: a scalpel, a set square, a bone (a bookbinder's special tool – a flat bone, slightly curved, used for polishing, rubbing and marking without making dents), an industrial precision vice, a file, a paring machine used for preparing the leather for binding, and a blocking press.

A book is made up of folded double-page spreads assembled into sections. After printing, the pages have to be folded and the sections collated. Tim then 'knocks them up' so that all the pages are accurately aligned – a tricky operation in such a small size – and glues the stitched sections together along the spine. Once the glue is dry the endpapers are put on. Next he sews the spine with cotton thread and a sharp needle, using a lock stitch. The book is then pressed in a vice. After this the top edge of the book is trimmed, using a scalpel, and gilded with gold foil applied with a heated gilding machine. The gold foil is backed with heat-soluble glue and simply rolled on. Next it has to be rounded and backed. The bone is used to round the edges of the spine to produce a slight curve which will fit well into the cover without any sharp angle. Finally the head and tail bands are added, hand-sewn in place at the top and bottom of the spine, to give extra strength and protection.

Marbled endpapers are the traditional way of adding a further decorative touch to a hand-bound book. Papers with a delicate

enough design for this purpose are scarce, but Tim eventually found a supplier who could provide hand-marbled papers where the design was detailed enough. Such papers are expensive, but one sheet will cut into hundreds of endpapers for the tiny books.

Lastly Tim makes the covers. The fine Indian silk he uses for the smaller, dolls' house editions is generally in a vivid shade of blue. It is difficult to work with because of a tendency to fray, but he feels it adds a final touch of luxury. For the leather-bound volumes, he uses the best-quality Moroccan goatskin, which has a more distinctive appearance than a smooth leather binding. Leather for bookbinding is specially cured and treated with vitamins to make it supple and to prevent it from decaying. It is quite thick, and has to be pared down using the paring machine, so that eventually the top surface of the leather, which is to be used for the book cover, is about the same thickness as photocopier paper. There is no margin for error in this skilled job, and as there is a great variation in the grain of each piece of leather, some pieces are more difficult to work with than others.

Before they are put on, the leather covers are decorated with gold foil. On a miniature book the cover design includes the title on the spine, which for a full-size book would be stamped on *after* the cover has been attached. Tim has a metal block made up to his design and uses the heated blocking press to imprint it on to the leather. It is always a difficult

Above *Flower Talk* – a pull-out book which is tremendously popular.

Below A rarity – a miniature bookpress with some of Tim's books. The bookpress was supplied by Hannah Roet.

operation: the grain of the leather can easily cause the gilding to smudge on to areas which are not intended to be gilded, and any excess has to be laboriously removed.

This complicated process is made more difficult by the scale. Indeed at any stage one slip means that all the work has been wasted and the book can be ruined. Tim is very careful, so wastage is rare, but on one sad occasion, just before a dolls' house fair where he was introducing a new title, he got one of the special limited editions ready for binding – and then dropped it into the glue pot!

One almost insoluble problem in binding miniature books is that is difficult to make the books stay closed. The long fibres in good quality paper act like a spring if they are bent. With full-size books the weight of the covers keeps the book closed, but with miniature books the weight is insufficient. As Allan did before him, Tim makes a small clip from brass foil for the leather-bound, collector's editions, bending it to shape with a pair of blunt-nosed pliers.

As every bibliophile knows, all books should be treated with care. Tim says there is a tendency for people to open a very tiny book by holding the top edges, and it is possible to damage the delicate gilding if it is handled repeatedly in this way. His books are as strongly bound as full-size books and, handled properly, will last indefinitely.

Terence Stringer
The Turner

Terence Stringer is a skilled turner specializing in exquisite decorative accessories, all in the standard dolls' house 1/12 scale. Some of his pieces are so tiny that it seems almost impossible that he produces everything on a full-size Coronet lathe, working at its maximum speed of 2,300rpm.

Terence is a self-taught turner and has gained his expertise through years of practice. He is also a trained silversmith, something he began to take his mind off his stressful job as operations manager of a bonded warehouse in London. He worked such long hours that his wife, Heather, complained that she never saw him. When she took up lacemaking as a hobby to pass the time while he was away at work, she asked Terence if he thought he could make her some bobbins. He bought a lathe and 50 blanks to make a start. Out of those 50 he successfully turned just four bobbins, and decided to buy her some instead. It was at that point that he abandoned woodwork – or so he thought – and took up silversmithing. Although his first attempt at a craft had not been a success, he found the second, his silversmithing, absorbing, and duly registered his mark, TGS, in 1976. His new-found skills and enjoyment of fine handwork finally led him to decide on a change of lifestyle. He gave up his job and they moved to Cornwall, though as yet with no clear idea of what he intended to do next.

He had always enjoyed studying antique furniture, and when he read an article in a crafts magazine about someone making quarter-scale furniture, he felt that he, too,

would like to have a go. He still had the lathe from his previous attempt at woodwork, and now with more time to concentrate, he set about teaching himself, slowly and methodically. After about six months' practice, taking one stage at a time and mastering each technique in turn, he succeeded in making a quarter-scale Windsor chair, copied from one belonging to a friend, and went on to make six more, using recycled elm and yew. When he decided to exhibit his chairs at a craft fair in Truro, the show was a success and his work was filmed and shown on local television.

Although the woodwork now seemed to be promising, Terence says that it was through making his silver jewellery that he really discovered how much he enjoyed work with very fine detail, and when he heard that there was to be a dolls' house and miniatures fair in Cornwall, the first to be held there, he began to think of moving down from 1/4 scale. His first essay into 1/12 scale was to make a replica of a gentleman's ebony dressing set, copying a full-size one he had bought at a local antiques market. For the materials he returned to the same market and bought an old ebony tray which provided enough wood to make plenty of miniatures.

Finding suitable bristles for the shaving brush was at first a problem: hair which feels very soft in a larger brush can seem harsh and scratchy when cut down to the small size. The solution was to use the finest bristle from a really high quality shaving brush, and although this might seem expensive, he points out that, as with the ebony, one full-size brush is enough for a great quantity of miniatures. He still makes 1/12 scale shaving brushes, and Heather cuts the bristles and embeds them into the wood a few at a time – very fiddly, time-consuming work.

Terence realized that he would need to make a range of items to display at the miniatures fair, so he used two lignum-vitae

Ebony candlestick with candle, lignum-vitae twist-stem hatstand and ebony walking cane with silver handle. The desk in the picture was one of the very first pieces of miniature furniture to be made by Geoffrey Wonnacott (*see* page 118).

bowls that he had bought in a market to make small turned items such as paperweights in the shape of apples and pears, and tobacco jars. For further variety, he made some ebony walking sticks with silver knobs. He has since increased the number of small accessories he makes in sterling silver – all hallmarked where practical, but often they are too small for this to be possible. The height of the letters in the smallest available mark is 1/50in (0.5mm), and stamping on the mark at the Assay office can bend the silver out of shape even when there is sufficient space.

Work on a hand mirror to complement the shaving brush was held up when he could not find a glass supplier – until eventually he found a fellow miniaturist who had been forced to buy 1/25in (1mm) mirror glass in quantity or not at all, which meant that he had far too much for his own work

169

and was pleased to let Terence buy some. Ken Palmer (*see* page 160) now cuts and bevels the glass for Terence's mirrors, and also supplies the tiny lens for his minute magnifying glass – which you can really see through if you try hard.

To his delight, people seemed to like his work and it sold well. He was also asked to supply things he had not made before, and this gave him the stimulus to study and experiment; each new addition to his range means that he has to spend a lot of time on the initial research. When he had enough variety of small items ready, Terence began to sell to dolls' house shops and his work snowballed. Once dolls' house collectors realize that such small accessories are actually available, they ask for more and more things. He studies period designs in museums and makes a bewildering number of sewing items, ranging from a darning mushroom in boxwood to a sterling silver thimble and a pin cushion in the shape of a shoe, copied from a Victorian one.

His bone knitting needles are ¹⁄₁₅in (0.5mm) thick by ⁷⁄₈in (23mm) long and he now has no trouble with lace bobbins – even though his miniature versions are ¹⁄₃₀in (0.8mm) thick by ⅜in (9mm) long. These are not intended to actually work on, he points out, as they are extremely fragile and delicate. Anyone who wants to add some 'work in progress' should use full-size lace bobbins to make a sample to transfer, while the best way to achieve miniature knitting is to use long dressmaker's pins and then slip the work on to the bone needles.

Terence is quite a big man with large hands, and I still find it extraordinary that he should be able to make such very tiny things with the same lathe as might be used for massive wooden bowls or full-size chair legs. He makes all his own turning tools by grinding down 4in (10cm) masonry nails to

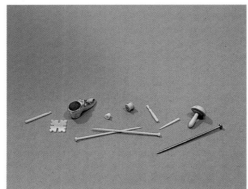

Above **A selection of miniature sewing equipment – compare the size with the dressmaker's pin on the right of the picture.**

Below **A bone rolling blotter and dip pen with a silver nib – the A4 writing paper gives an indication of scale.**

exactly the same shapes as he would use in full size, but recommends that anyone wanting to use this technique should fit them into a wooden handle for safety. You need to be able to work with the tool in one hand and with the fingers of the other acting as a 'steady' to stop the fine article from flexing, he explains; you also need to keep hold of the article when parting off, if it is not to fly away and disappear. Tools have to be razor sharp all the time – this is essential to success. Terence stops every 10 or 15 minutes, depending on which material he is using, to sharpen them. Tools which are not sharp enough are often a real handicap for amateurs, he says, as they have to force the tool into the material rather than let it cut. This is important enough for large-scale work; for the miniaturist it is vital.

Although he uses a magnifier on an Anglepoise stand over the lathe, he says he really works by feeling what is happening rather than seeing it, and that after a while this becomes second nature. Miniature turning is something you have to teach yourself, because anyone trying to demonstrate the techniques will be covering up most of the work with their hand. Even so, Terence says he needs to check with his magnifier, because many people who buy his minute turned accessories take them home and then inspect them through their own. If he worked without one, he might miss tiny flaws that would be visible to his customers.

Terence doesn't spend all his time turning; he handcarves his twist-stem hatstand, cutting the spiral first with a junior hacksaw, and then broadening it out with a needle file. Smaller spirals, for a candlestick, are cut initially with a razor saw. And for a relatively restful change, he will spend a day silversmithing – he likes to alternate his work for variety.

Terence and Heather have finally settled down in Norfolk, in a peaceful spot on the edge of a village which is still well off the beaten track, but rather more accessible than Cornwall. They exhibit at 12 miniatures fairs each year, and realized that travelling from the far south-west was taking up too much working time, as they need to be able to go to London, the Midlands or the north of England without having to spend too many nights away from home.

A visit to Strangers' Hall in Norwich stimulated Terence's interest in period toys, especially as the museum curator helped by getting things out of storage so that he could study them, and trips to the museum are now a regular occurrence. Dolls' house nurseries are a rich field for the collector and Terence is developing his range of decorative toys and tiny boxes. Bilboquet, the ball-and-cup game which is said to have been Jane Austen's favourite, is one. Diablo, the 'devil-on-two-sticks', is another once popular game. Some of his other toys are based on modern souvenirs brought back from holidays abroad or given as presents, like the tiny sets of Russian dolls, or a Russian doll egg with a tiny flower egg nestling inside. Heather paints these using acrylic paints, so these little toys are unpolished. Other turned items are are all wax polished on the lathe. This skill is something acquired with long practice in 1/12 scale work – Terence says you get to know exactly how much pressure you can put on such miniscule objects without breaking them.

Sets of skittles might seem an ideal game for the miniature household, but for Terence they presented a problem – turning a

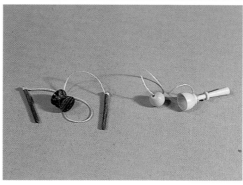

Top **Original boxes, painted by Heather Stringer. The circus tent is supplied complete with ringmaster and clown. The cat boxes are favourites with Japanese collectors.**

Above **Copies of two antique toys: diablo and the ball-and-cup game.**

Below **A row of skittle dolls, each ⅞in (23mm) or less tall.**

set of undecorated skittles with every one identical is almost impossible in this size. But people kept asking for skittles, and when he discovered that in the past skittles were painted with decorative patterns, he hit on the idea of providing them painted as an individual character, like a doll. Heather, with her City and Guilds qualifications in fashion and design, and her trained painting skills, felt she could help with those, and as a result they have become tremendously popular. Terence plans to repeat this idea with a Noah's Ark set, producing the pairs of animals at regular intervals, and has already studied old Noah's Ark sets in Bethnal Green Museum of Childhood.

Terence recalls that it was originally pressure of work which caused him to take up his new occupation, so that he could be his own master and work at his own pace. In fact, he now still works long hours, beginning at 8:30 a.m. each morning and finishing at around 6:30 p.m., but there is time for a lunch-break and once he has finished for the evening his time is his own – in general. Completing a special order or making enough stock to exhibit at a miniatures fair is a different matter. Before a deadline, Terence and Heather generally find themselves working into the night. On one occasion they actually got to bed at 2:15 a.m. and had to get up at 4:00 a.m. to go to a show. But this is the exception, and, fortunately, not a frequent occurrence.

John Hodgson
The Master

For the past five years, one of our finest miniaturists, John Hodgson, has been working on a collection of miniature houses commissioned by John Guthrie, the owner of Hever Castle in Kent. The Guthrie Miniature Model House Collection forms a display illustrating life in English country houses from mediaeval to Georgian times. John is well known both in England and America for his exceptionally fine period furniture, and has now produced three outstanding houses to contain a collection of both his own work and that of other leading miniaturists in Britain, many of whom are featured in this book.

We include the Georgian house from the collection to illustrate John's outstanding craftmanship as a maker both of dolls' houses and furniture, and the extraordinary skill of the other miniaturists involved in this undertaking.

John Hodgson was born in South Africa. His family lived in a remote area, and as a

child he spent a good deal of time on his own, amusing himself by drawing, carving pieces of wood, and generally making things with his hands.

John moved with his family to England, and eventually, after art college and marriage, decided to try his hand at making miniature furniture.

After a modest start exhibiting at a local show, the rapid success of his work in the United States encouraged John to take up making miniature furniture as a full-time occupation. With his wife, Sue, as secretary and 'organizer' he now has a thriving business to run.

John believes that his interest in art helps him to achieve the correct proportion in 1/12 scale, which is not always simply a matter of reducing the piece from a full-size drawing. It is essential to have a good 'eye' if the miniature is to look exactly right.

He particularly loves making chairs, with all the associated handcarving of cabriole legs, ball-and-claw feet, shell motifs and intricate backsplats, but his favourite furniture generally is William and Mary and Queen Anne walnut pieces. He uses carefully selected burr walnut veneer to ensure that the figuring and cross-graining of the wood is as authentic as possible in miniature scale.

John prefers to use old wood, as this has the fine grain needed for authenticity. The grain has to be straight and the wood solid, and old tables with walnut or mahogany leaves are a good source of raw material.

John's work is stunning, and the pictures reproduced on the following pages are a testament to his quite extraordinary achievement.

The Georgian country house (*see* opposite) built by John Hodgson is typical of the period 1720–80. The house comprises the main hall, staircase and top landing, dining room, library, and a drawing room and bedroom. The latter can only be seen through the windows, to avoid spoiling the facade of the house.

The entrance hall, staircase and landing can be seen in the photograph on this page. The Palladian-style staircase provides an impressive frontage to the house, with a lofty gallery of columns in the centre at the top of the stairs. The elegant symmetry for which Georgian houses are noted is evident in the arrangement of gilt half-console tables, mirrors and chairs, and the *torchères* holding a pair of Ming-style lidded jars. All the Ming-style porcelain in the hall is by Muriel Hopwood (*see* page 142). Each example is a hand-painted, accurate copy of an original piece.

The stairway, with its painted and gilt balustrades, is framed by the marble columns in the foreground, and the doors to rooms leading off are made from solid mahogany. To the left is the dining room, and at the top of the stairs, the library.

The portraits, which are all copies of original paintings, are in oils on silk, by Michael Taylor. In the centre of the back wall is *Lady Eglington* (Reynolds), on the left is *Earl Grosvenor's Bandy* (Stubbs) and on the right *Laetitia, Lady Lade* (Stubbs).

The figures, by David Hoyles, portray servants bringing in the chest of the son of the house, who has just returned from war.

The dining room (this page) is painted in Pompeiian red, a colour that enjoyed great popularity in the Georgian period. This bold background sets off the pictures and mirrors in their gilt frames beautifully. The painting over the heavily carved mantelpiece is of Johann Jakob Astor, copied by Michael Taylor from an original by Gilbert Stuart, which hangs in Hever Castle.

The mahogany four-pedestal table is 16½in (420mm) long, and is set with a bone china dinner service by Karen Griffiths. The pattern is a derivation of the Greek key design, a classical motif that was popular during the eighteenth century. The dinner service is monogrammed with the letter 'G' for Guthrie.

Also on the table is hallmarked silverware by Ken Palmer (wine coolers, and *see* page 160), Josie Studd (tableware), and Stuart McCabe (salts with spoons), exquisite handblown glassware by Edward Hill (*see* page 130), and fruit by Christine Lincoln. The sideboard, which has been made especially to fit into the alcove, also holds further silverware and glass.

The twelve mahogany Chippendale-style chairs round the table are only 3in (75mm) high, with a fine interwoven design in each back-splat. Around the sides of the room are chairs in the Chinese Chippendale style, and half-console tables under the mirrors which are topped with grey Devon marble, to match the Corinthian columns with their gold-leaved capitals.

The carpets, by Patricia Borwick, are of a typical Georgian design, and the chandelier is made to an eighteenth-century design, by Donald and Robert Ward.

Around the room are examples of porcelain by Muriel Hopwood. The blue-and-orange floral pieces are typical eighteenth-century export platters, based on one at Sudbury Hall in Derbyshire. The hand-painted lidded jars are oriental in style.

In the book-lined library (left), the young soldier, dressed as an officer of Battalion Company, 5th Regiment, tells his parents of his adventures in the war.

Over the mantelpiece is *The James Family* (Arthur Devis), by Michael Taylor. The crystal chandelier is by Donald and Robert Ward, and the blue-and-white porcelain by Muriel Hopwood.

The library contains a set of six mahogany ribbon-back Chippendale-style chairs, upholstered in fabric hand-embroidered in flame-stitch by Patricia Borwick. One of these chairs can be seen to the right of the picture.

On the mantelpiece is a pair of silver Corinthian column-style candlesticks, *circa* 1770, by Stuart McCabe.

In the drawing room, French-style gilt furniture and English Chippendale-style mahogany and marble give a superb impression of the luxurious lifestyle of the Georgian nobility.

The eighteenth-century French armchair and footstool (below) are upholstered in fine silk.

The breakfront mahogany bookcase (above) is 10in (25.5cm) long, has three astragal doors, and contains a collection of books and porcelain. The porcelain, by Muriel Hopwood, consists of different designs of fifteenth- and sixteenth-century Ming-style dishes, and some 'kraak'-style deep plates. Books are kept on either side, and below are three cupboards.

The furniture found in the bedroom has the simple, elegant lines that characterize the Georgian period. The mahogany linen press (left), used to store larger items, has shelves at the top for linen, and drawers beneath. The edges are carved with a flower-and-dart design, and there are cockbeaded edges on all drawers.

The mahogany four-poster bed (below) is the centrepiece of the bedroom. It has fielded panels on the backboard and tester (the 'roof'), and the top frieze is heavily carved with the gadroon pattern, an inverted curved design which was very popular at the time. The bed covers, cushion and hangings are silk with gold braiding, with a gathered valance around the base. There is a leather-bound book of prayers on the bed.

The mahogany graduated chest of drawers (right) is in the Chinese Chippendale style. On top of the chest a lady's wig rests on its stand, and her silver brush, comb and mirror are ready to hand. This set of silverware, and the inkwell, are by Ken Palmer.

Bibliography

Banister, Judith *Old English Silver*, Evans Brothers Ltd., 1965

Banister, Manly *Bookbindng as a Handcraft*, Sterling, New York, 1975

Battie, David (Ed.) *Sotheby's Concise Encyclopaedia of Porcelain*, Conran Octopus, 1990

Bedford, J.R. *A Basic Course of Practical Metalwork*, John Murray, 1960

Bracken Books *Lacquer: An International History and Collector's Guide*, Crowood Press, 1984, new edition, Bracken Books, 1989

Bradley, Elizabeth *Decorative Victorian Needlework*, Ebury Press, 1990

Brunskill, Ronald and
Clifton–Taylor, Alec *English Brickwork*, Ward Lock, 1977

Clifton–Taylor, Alec *The Pattern of English Building*, Faber & Faber, 1972

Davenport, John *Making Miniature Furniture*, Batsford, 1988

Forman, Benno M. *American Seating Furniture 1630–1730* The Winterthur Museum, 1988, W.W. Norton & Co. Inc. New York

Gay, John *Cast Iron*, John Murray, 1985

Hayward, Helena (Ed.) *World Furniture*, Paul Hamlyn, 1965

Hillier, Mary *Automata and Mechanical Toys*, Jupiter, 1976

Innes, Jocasta *Scandinavian Painted Decor*, Cassell, 1990

Jackson, Valerie *Dolls' Houses and Miniatures*, John Murray, 1988

Klein, Dan and Lloyd, Ward *The History of Glass*, Orbis Publications, 1984

Loyen, Frances *The Thames & Hudson Manual of Silversmithing*, 1980

MacQuoid, Percy *A History of English Furniture*, Bracken Books, 1988

Manners, Errol *Ceramic Source Book*, Collins & Brown, 1990

Marshall, Jo *Glass Source Book*, Chartwell Books Inc., 1990

Payne, Christopher (Ed.) *Sotheby's Concise Encyclopaedia of Furniture*, Conran Octopus Publications, 1989

Poliakoff, Miranda *Silver Toys and Miniatures*, Victoria & Albert Museum Publications

Priestley J.B. *The Prince of Pleasure and His Regency 1811–20*, William Heinemann, 1969

Sainsbury, John *Turning Miniatures in Wood*, GMC Publications, 1986

Salazar, Tristan *The Complete Book of Furniture Restoration*, Bison Books, 1980

Shaker *Shaker Handbook of Furniture*, Shaker, London,

Sparkes, Ivan G. *Early Windsor Chairs*, Shire Books,

Symonds, R.W. *Masterpieces of English Furniture and Clocks*, Batsford, 1940, new edition, Studio Editions, 1980

Wilson, Michael I. *The English Country House and Its Furnishings*, Batsford, 1977

Addresses

Names and addresses of the craftspeople included in this book are presented in alphabetical order. Please enclose a stamped addressed envelope with any enquiry.

Gordon Blacklock
18 Countisbury Road
Norton
Stockton
Cleveland TS20 1PZ

Black Country Miniatures
63 Church Street,
Halesowen,
West Midlands B62 9LQ

David Booth
16 Narrabeen Road
Cheriton
Folkestone
Kent CT19 4DD

Jeremy Collins
(Gable End Designs)
'Gable End'
190 Station Road
Knowle
Solihull
West Midlands B93 0ER

John Davenport
'Appledore'
211 Botley Road
Burridge
Southampton S03 7BJ

Ann Davey
Easton House
Pound Lane
Easton
Wells
Somerset BA5 1EF

Josie and Danny
Drinkwater
(Tetbury Miniatures)
Gordon House
12 Silver Street
Tetbury
Glos GL8 8DH

Judith Dunger
11 Lyndale
Stevenage
Herts SG1 1UB

Edward Hill
(Glassblowing of
Greenwich)
324 Creek Road
Greenwich
London SE10 9SW

Denis Hillman
3 Shipley Lane
Cooden
Bexhill-on-Sea
East Sussex TN39 3SR

Michelle Hipkins
(Acorn Tapestries)
'Bleak House'
Church Street
Highley
Shropshire WV16 6NA

Barry Hipwell
123 Park Road
Loughborough
Leics LE11 2HD

John Hodgson
26 Sands Lane
Bridlington
North Humberside
YO15 2JG

Muriel Hopwood
41 Eastbourne Avenue
Hodge Hill
Birmingham B34 6AR

Charlotte Hunt
31 Westover Road
London SW18 2RE

Carol Lodder
(Belchalwell Pottery)
Brooks Cottage
Belchalwell
Blandford Forum
Dorset DT11 0EG

Jim Martyn
(Modelscape)
7 Leaches Buildings
Boundary Road
Newark
Notts NG24 4BA

Peter Mattinson
100 Stockton Lane
York
North Yorks Y03 0BU

Alan McKirdy
Chapel Green
Long Melford
Sudbury
Suffolk CO10 9HX

Michael and Edwards
   Partners
East Farm
Edderside
Maryport
Cumbria CA15 6RA

Reg Miller
12 Springhurst Road
Shipley
West Yorks BD18 3DN

John and Jean Morgan
(Simply Shaker)
86 Oaklands Avenue
Watford WD1 4LW

Mulvany & Rogers
2 South Lane
Kingston-on-Thames
Surrey KT1 2NJ

Ken Palmer
The Courtyard
Pipe Grange Farm
Lichfield Road
Pipe Hill
Lichfield
Staffs WS13 8JP

Patrick Puttock
The Old Crown Inn
Lopen
Near South Petherton
Somerset TA13 5JX

Colin and Yvonne
   Roberson
10 Portobello Close
Chesham
Bucks HP5 2PL

Gordon and Joyce Rossiter
(Rosscraft)
7 Little Britain
Dorchester
Dorset DT1 1NN

Brian and Eileen Rumble
(Rudeigin Beag)
Strawberrybank Cottage
Backmuir of Liff
by Dundee DD2 5QU
Scotland

Tim Sheppard
(Lilliput Press)
10 Manor Road
Bishopston
Bristol BS7 8PY

Terence Stringer
Spindles
Lexham Road
Litcham
Norfolk PE32 2QQ

Robert Stubbs
12 Pebble View Walk
Hopton-on-Sea
Great Yarmouth
Norfolk NR31 9SG

Bernardo Traettino
33 Hertford Avenue
East Sheen
London SW14 8EF

Ivan Turner
13 Westmorland Drive
Durdham Park
Bristol BS6 6XH

John Watkins
12 Biddel Springs
Highworth
Swindon
Wilts SN6 7BH

Trevor Webster
(Vale Dolls House)
'Wayside'
Church Street
Whatton in the Vale
Notts NG13 9EL

Geoffrey Wonnacott
12 Ford Crescent
Bradworthy
Holsworthy
Devon EX22 7QR

Ellie Yannas
36 Westbridge Road
London SW11 3PW

Dolls' House and Miniatures Magazines

Britain

Dolls House and Miniature Scene
(bi-monthly, on general sale)
EMF Publishing
5 Cissbury Road
Ferring
West Sussex BN12 6QJ
0903 506626

Dolls House World
(bi-monthly, subscription)
Ashdown Publishing Ltd
Shelley House
104 High Street
Steyning
West Sussex BN4 3RD
0903 815622

The Home Miniaturist
(bi-monthly, subscription)
Ashdown Publishing Ltd
(see above)

The Miniatures Catalogue of Great Britain
(on general sale)
Ashdown Publishing Ltd
(see above)

International Dolls' House News
(quarterly, subscription)
IDHN Publishing
PO Box 154
Cobham
Surrey KT11 2YE
0932 860607

The British Dolls' House Hobby Directory is an annually updated publication of approximately 116 pages, published in May each year; it contains the names and addresses of over 250 makers and suppliers of dolls' house miniatures, dolls' house fairs and shops, and gives subscription details of dolls' house magazines. It costs £3 plus a strong A5 SAE stamped for 250g from:
LDF Publications
25 Priory Road
Kew
Richmond
Surrey TW9 3DQ

United States

Nutshell News
(monthly, subscription)
Kalmbach Miniatures Inc.
PO Box 1612
Waukesha
WI 53187

Miniatures Catalog
(annual)
Kalmbach Miniatures Inc.
(see above)

Places to Visit

Objects which inspired the craftspeople featured in this book can be found at the addresses below. Please telephone to check opening hours before making a journey.

American Museum
 in Britain
Claverton Manor
Near Bath
Avon
0222 460503
✦ John and Jean Morgan

Blakesley Hall
Blakesley Road
Yardley
Birmingham
021 783 2193
✦ Barry Hipwell

Charleston Farmhouse
Firle, Near Lewes
East Sussex
0323 811265
✦ Carol Lodder

Fairfax House
Castlegate
York
0904 655543
✦ Barry Hipwell

Harewood House
Leeds
West Yorkshire
0532 886225
✦ Geoffrey Wonnacott

Hever Castle
The Guthrie Collection
 of Miniature Model
 Houses
Hever
Near Edenbridge
Kent
0732 865224
✦ John Hodgson

The Lock Museum
54 New Road
Willenhall
West Midlands
0902 634542
✦ Barry Hipwell

The Museum of London
London Wall
London EC2
071 600 3699
✦ Ivan Turner

Newarke Houses Museum
The Newarke
Leicester
0533 554100
✦ Barry Hipwell

Percival David Foundation
 of Chinese Art
(University of London,
School of Oriental &
African Studies)
53 Gordon Square
London WC1
071 387 3909
✦ Muriel Hopwood

Puppen and Spielzug
8803 Rothenburg
o.d. Tauber
Hofbronnengasse 13
Germany
✦ Charlotte Hunt

The Red Lodge
Park Row
Bristol
0272 299771
✦ Ivan Turner

The Royal Pavilion
Brighton
East Sussex
0273 603005
✦ Colin and
Yvonne Roberson

The Science Museum
Exhibition Road
South Kensington
London SW7
071 589 3456
✦ Ivan Turner

Strangers' Hall
Charing Cross
Norwich
Norfolk
0603 611277
✦ Terence Stringer

The Victoria & Albert
 Museum
Cromwell Road
South Kensington
London SW7
071 589 6371
✦ Carol Lodder
✦ Ivan Turner

Weald and Downland
 Open Air Museum
Singleton
West Sussex
024 363 348
✦ Trevor Webster

184
✦ Carol Lodder

Some of the author's favourite sources of information

The Bowes Museum
Barnard Castle
Co. Durham
0833 690606
Famous silver swan automaton

Dartington Crystal
Great Torrington
North Devon
0805 24233
For tours of factory to see glass being blown and made

Fenton House
Hampstead Grove
Hampstead
London NW3
071 435 2471
Collection of early keyboard instruments

Number One,
  Royal Crescent
Bath
0225 428126
A Georgian house furnished in period

Nunnington Hall
(The National Trust)
Near Helmsley
North Yorkshire
043 95 283
The Carlisle Collection of Miniature Rooms

Pickford's House Museum
41 Friar Gate
Derby
0332 293111
A Georgian house furnished with good plain furniture

Dyrham Park
(The National Trust)
Near Bath and Bristol
0272 299771
A William and Mary house with much blue-and-white porcelain

Bristol Museum and
  Art Gallery
Queen's Road
Bristol
0272 299771
Bristol blue glass; fine pottery

Oxford University Museum
Parks Road
Oxford
0865 272950
Cast-iron columns with wrought iron decoration

In addition, to see outstanding work by leading miniaturists:

The Doll House
42 Bourne Street
London SW1
071 730 4046
(by appointment only)

A World in Miniature
North Pier
Oban
Argyll
Scotland
085 26 272

Carol and Barry Kaye's
  Museum of Miniature Art
5900 Wilshire Boulevard
(East Wing)
Los Angeles
CA 90036
USA

Angels Attic
516 Colorado Avenue
Santa Monica
CA 90401
USA

Metric Conversion Table

Inches to Millimetres and Centimetres

MM – millimetres   CM – Centimetres

Inches	MM	CM	Inches	CM	Inches	CM
⅛	3	0.3	9	22.9	30	76.2
¼	6	0.6	10	25.4	31	78.7
⅜	10	1.0	11	27.9	32	81.3
½	13	1.3	12	30.5	33	83.8
⅝	16	1.6	13	33.0	34	86.4
¾	19	1.9	14	35.6	35	88.9
⅞	22	2.2	15	38.1	36	91.4
1	25	2.5	16	40.6	37	94.0
1¼	32	3.2	17	43.2	38	96.5
1½	38	3.8	18	45.7	39	99.1
1¾	44	4.4	19	48.3	40	101.6
2	51	5.1	20	50.8	41	104.1
2½	64	6.4	21	53.3	42	106.7
3	76	7.6	22	55.9	43	109.2
3½	89	8.9	23	58.4	44	111.8
4	102	10.2	24	61.0	45	114.3
4½	114	11.4	25	63.5	46	116.8
5	127	12.7	26	66.0	47	119.4
6	152	15.2	27	68.6	48	121.9
7	178	17.8	28	71.1	49	124.5
8	203	20.3	29	73.7	50	127.0

Index

About the Author

Jean Nisbett began to take notice of period houses, their decoration and furniture before she was 10 years old, and they have been a consuming passion ever since. While bringing up a family she turned this interest to the miniature scale, and restored, decorated and furnished many dolls' houses. Her houses have been shown on Channel 4 and BBC television.

She began writing while working in the London offices of an American advertising agency, and is well-known as the leading British writer in the dolls' house field. Her articles have appeared regularly in the specialist miniatures and dolls' house magazines since 1985, as well as in home decoration magazines. Jean Nisbett lives in Bath.

Other Titles available from GMC Publications Limited

Books

Woodworking Plans and Projects GMC Publications
40 More Woodworking Plans and Projects GMC Publications
Woodworking Crafts Annual GMC Publications
Turning Miniatures in Wood John Sainsbury
Woodcarving: A Complete Course Ron Butterfield
Pleasure and Profit from Woodturning Reg Sherwin
Making Unusual Miniatures Graham Spalding
Furniture Projects for the Home Ernest Parrott
Seat Weaving Ricky Holdstock
Green Woodwork Mike Abbott
The Incredible Router Jeremy Broun
Electric Woodwork Jeremy Broun
Woodturning: A Foundation Course Keith Rowley
Upholstery: A Complete Course David James
Upholstery: Techniques and Projects David James
Making Shaker Furniture Barry Jackson
The Complete Dolls' House Book Jean Nisbett
Making Dolls' House Furniture Patricia King
Making Tudor Dolls' Houses Derek Rowbottom
Making Georgian Dolls' Houses Derek Rowbottom
Making Period Dolls' House Furniture Derek & Sheila Rowbottom
Heraldic Miniature Knights Peter Greenhill
Furniture Projects Rod Wales
Restoring Rocking Horses Clive Green & Anthony Dew
Making Fine Furniture: Projects Tom Darby
Making & Modifying Woodworking Tools Jim Kingshott
The Workshop Jim Kingshott
Sharpening: The Complete Guide Jim Kingshott
Multi-Centre Woodturning Ray Hopper
Woodturning Wizardry David Springett
Complete Woodfinishing Ian Hosker
Making Little Boxes from Wood John Bennett
Decorative Woodcarving Jeremy Williams
Making Wooden Toys Terry Kelly
Turning Wooden Toys Terry Lawrence
Woodcarving Tools, Materials & Equipment Chris Pye
Members' Guide to Marketing Jack Pigden
Woodworkers' Career and Educational Source Book GMC Publications

GMC Publications regularly produces new books on a wide range of woodworking and craft subjects,
and an increasing number of specialist magazines, all available on subscription

Magazines

Woodturning ✦ *Woodcarving* ✦ *Business Matters*

All these books and magazines are available through bookshops and newsagents, or may be ordered by post
from the publishers at 166 High Street, Lewes, East Sussex BN7 1XU, telephone (0273) 477374.
Credit card orders are accepted. Please write or phone for the latest information.